the
ANTIQUE DEALERS
pocketbook

While every care has been taken in the compiling of information contained in this volume the publishers cannot accept any liability for loss, financial or otherwise, incurred by reliance placed on the information herein.

ISBN 0-86248-025-6

INTRODUCTION

With the ever increasing popularity of antique collecting, there is a need for a comprehensive reference book containing detailed illustrations – not only of the items which command the highest prices but also those pieces which, although not antiques in the true sense, are much sought after by members of the trade.

Here, in one handy, pocket sized volume, are well over 2,000 clear illustrations to facilitate instant recognition and dating of the host of day to day items which make up the bulk of the antique market.

Compiled primarily with the professional dealer in view, this book makes inter-trade reference simple and accurate.

Interior decorators too, will find communication with their clients considerably improved through use of this book, once again ensuring that there can be no confusion resulting from verbal descriptions being inaccurately given or incompletely understood.

We are confident that every user of The Antique Dealer's Pocket Book will find it of invaluable assistance in the smooth running of his business and a useful addition to his works of reference.

TONY CURTIS

Hazell Watson & Viney Ltd, Aylesbury, Bucks

CONTENTS

Monarchs. 6
Chinese Dynasties 6
Periods 7
Registry of Designs 7
China Marks 8
Handles 10
Pediments 10
Legs 11
Feet 11
Chair Backs 12
Barometers. 13
Bronze 13
Caddies & Boxes 14
Cameras. 14
Cane Handles 15
Carved Wood 15
China 16-34
    Oriental. 35-40
Clocks. 41-50
Copper & Brass 51
Dolls. 52
Furniture. 53-104
    Armoires 53
    Beds 54
    Bookcases 55
    Bureaux. 56
    Bureau Bookcases 57
    Cabinets 58
    Canterburys 59
    Chairs, Dining. 60
        Easy 61
        Elbow. 62
    Chests of Drawers 63
    Chest on Chest 64
    Chest on Stand 65
    Chiffoniers 66
    Coffers & Trunks. 67
    Commode Chests. 68
    Commodes & Pot Cupboards. 69
    Corner Cupboards 70
    Court Cupboards. 71
    Cradles 72
    Credenzas 73
    Cupboards 74
    Davenports. 75
    Display Cabinets 76
    Dressers. 77
    Dumb Waiters. 78
    Hall Stands. 78
    Jardinieres 78

Lowboys 78
Pedestal & Kneehole Desks 79
Screens 80
Secretaires & Escritoires 81
Secretaire Bookcases 82
Settees & Couches 83
Shelves 84
Steps. 84
Sideboards 85
Stools 86
Suites 87
Tables 88
    Card & Tea. 88
    Consol. 89
    Dining. 90
    Dressing. 91
    Drop-Leaf 92
    Gateleg 93
    Large 94
    Occasional 95
    Pembroke 96
    Side 96
    Sofa 97
    Sutherland 97
    Workboxes & Games 98
    Writing Tables. 99
Teapoys. 100
Torcheres. 100
Towel Rails 100
Umbrella Stands 100
Wardrobes 101
Washstands. 102
Whatnots 103
Wine Coolers 104
Glass. 105-123
Instruments 124
Iron 125
Ivory. 125
Jade 126
Lead 126
Marble. 126
Mirrors 126
Money Banks 126
Musical Instruments 126
Pewter. 127
Pianos 127
Shibayama 127
Silver 128-154
Toys 155
Index 156

MONARCHS

HENRY IV	1399 – 1413	COMMONWEALTH	1649 – 1660
HENRY V	1413 – 1422	CHARLES II	1660 – 1685
HENRY VI	1422 – 1461	JAMES II	1685 – 1689
EDWARD IV	1461 – 1483	WILLIAM & MARY	1689 – 1695
EDWARD V	1483 – 1483	WILLIAM III	1695 – 1702
RICHARD III	1483 – 1485	ANNE	1702 – 1714
HENRY VII	1485 – 1509	GEORGE I	1714 – 1727
HENRY VIII	1509 – 1547	GEORGE II	1727 – 1760
EDWARD VI	1547 – 1553	GEORGE III	1760 – 1820
MARY	1553 – 1558	GEORGE IV	1820 – 1830
ELIZABETH	1558 – 1603	WILLIAM IV	1830 – 1837
JAMES I	1603 – 1625	VICTORIA	1837 – 1901
CHARLES I	1625 – 1649	EDWARD VII	1901 – 1910

CHINESE DYNASTIES

Shang	1766 – 1123BC	*5 Dynasties*	907 – 960
Zhou	1122 – 249BC	*Liao*	907 – 1125
Warring States	403 – 221BC	*Song*	960 – 1279
Qin	221 – 207BC	*Jin*	1115 – 1234
Han	206BC – AD220	*Yuan*	1260 – 1368
6 Dynasties	317 – 589	*Ming*	1368 – 1644
Sui	590 – 618	*Qing*	1644 – 1911
Tang	618 – 906		

REIGN PERIODS

MING

Hongwu	1368 – 1398	*Hongzhi*	1488 – 1505
Jianwen	1399 – 1402	*Zhengde*	1506 – 1521
Yongle	1403 – 1424	*Jiajing*	1522 – 1566
Hongxi	1425	*Longqing*	1567 – 1572
Xuande	1426 – 1435	*Wanli*	1573 – 1620
Zhengtong	1436 – 1449	*Taichang*	1620
Jingtai	1450 – 1456	*Tianqi*	1621 – 1627
Tianshun	1457 – 1464	*Chongzheng*	1628 – 1644
Chenghua	1465 – 1487		

QING

Shunzhi	1644 – 1662	*Daoguang*	1821 – 1850
Kangxi	1662 – 1722	*Xianfeng*	1851 – 1861
Yongzheng	1723 – 1735	*Tongzhi*	1862 – 1874
Qianlong	1736 – 1795	*Guangxu*	1875 – 1908
Jiali	1796 – 1820	*Xuantong*	1908 – 1911

PERIODS

TUDOR PERIOD	1485 – 1603	GEORGIAN PERIOD	1714 – 1820
ELIZABETHAN PERIOD	1558 – 1603	T. CHIPPENDALE	1715 – 1762
INIGO JONES	1572 – 1652	LOUIS XV PERIOD	1723 – 1774
JACOBEAN PERIOD	1603 – 1688	A. HEPPLEWHITE	1727 – 1788
STUART PERIOD	1603 – 1714	ADAM PERIOD	1728 – 1792
A. C. BOULLE	1642 – 1732	ANGELICA KAUFMANN	1741 – 1807
LOUIS XIV PERIOD	1643 – 1715	T. SHERATON	1751 – 1806
GRINLING GIBBONS	1648 – 1726	LOUIS XVI	1774 – 1793
CROMWELLIAN PERIOD	1649 – 1660	T. SHEARER	circa 1780
CAROLEAN PERIOD	1660 – 1685	REGENCY PERIOD	1800 – 1830
WILLIAM KENT	1684 – 1748	EMPIRE PERIOD	1804 – 1815
WILLIAM & MARY PERIOD	1689 – 1702	VICTORIAN PERIOD	1830 – 1901
QUEEN ANNE PERIOD	1702 – 1714	EDWARDIAN PERIOD	1901 – 1910

REGISTRY OF DESIGNS

USED 1842 to 1883

BELOW ARE ILLUSTRATED THE TWO FORM OF 'REGISTRY OF
DESIGN' MARK USED BETWEEN THE YEARS OF 1842 to 1883.

EXAMPLE: An article produced
between 1842 and 1867 would bear
the following marks. (Example for
the 12th of November 1852).

EXAMPLE: An article produced
between 1868 and 1883 would bear
the following marks. (Example for
the 22nd of October 1875).

DATE AND LETTER CODE

Month								
January	C	1842	X	54	J	66	Q	78	D
February	G	43	H	55	E	67	T	79	Y
March	W	44	C	56	L	68	X	80	J
April	H	45	A	57	K	69	H	81	E
May	E	46	I	58	B	70	O	82	L
June	M	47	F	59	M	71	A	83	K
July	I	48	U	60	Z	72	I		
August	R	49	S	61	R	73	F		
September	D	50	V	62	O	74	U		
October	B	51	P	63	G	75	S		
November	K	52	D	64	N	76	V		
December	A	53	Y	65	W	77	P		

CHINA MARKS

BELLEEK
1857 onwards

BLOOR DERBY
1815-1840

BLOOR DERBY

FRANKENTHAL
1755-1800

blue
1756

blue
1756-1759

blue
1762-1793

blue
1771

BOW
1750-1776

1750   1760   1770

HOCHST
1750-1798

red
1750-1762

blue
1762-1796

1765-1774

impressed
1760-1765

CAUGHLEY
1772-1814

Hf   *S*   *C*   SALOPIAN

imitation
Worcester   in blue   in blue   impressed

LEEDS
1760-1878

Hartley, Greens & Co
LEEDS POTTERY
1760-1783

LEEDS POTTERY
LEEDS POTTERY

impressed 1864

CHELSEA
1745-1784

Chelsea 1745

incised
1745-1749

in relief
1750-1753

red
1755

gold
1758-1770

MARTIN BROS
1873-1915

Martin Bros   R.W. MARTIN & BROS

London & Southall
1873   1900

COLEBROOK DALE
1785-1820

C Dale.   *Coalport*

1785-1820

MASONS
1795-1854

MASONS
PATENT IRONSTONE CHINA

FENTON
STONE WORKS

COPELAND
1847

COPELAND & GARRETT
1833

1847   1847-1891

COPELAND & CARR
NEW
FAYENCE
C.T.

1833-1847

MEISSON
1713

1713-1724   1725-1750   modern

DAVENPORT
1793-1882

Davenport

DAVENPORT
LONGPORT
STAFFORDSHIRE

DAVENPORTS
STONE CHINA

MENNECY
1734-1748

DV   *D.V.*

incised   in blue

MINTON
1793 onwards

X.   1851   MINTON
1800-1836   1860-1880

MINTON B B New Stone   MINTONS
1861 onward   20th century

DERBY
1745 onwards

D
1750
1750   1760   1770-1780

NANTGARW
1811-1820

Nantgarw   NANTGARW
1811   1813

DOULTON
1815

DOULTON
LAMBETH

DOULTON
LAMBETH

DOULTON
GROUP

pre 1836   1872

SWANSEA
NANGARW
1814

NANT GARW
O.W.
1816-1820

8

RECOGNITION & DATING - SOME USEFUL HINTS

Obviously the task of committing every china mark to memory is one which will be outside the scope of most collectors and, indeed, most dealers too. For this reason, the following simple guides may prove to be of some assistance in determining the approximate date of a piece without having recourse to long, and frequently involved, lists of the marks used by various manufacturers over the years.

Any piece bearing the words 'English Bone China' or simply 'Bone China' is a product of the twentieth century and the words 'Made in England' also suggest twentieth century manufacture, though they could relate to pieces dating from 1875 onward.

The word 'England' stamped on a piece suggests compliance with the McKinley Tariff Act of America, 1891 which required all imports to America to bear the name of the country of origin.

In 1862, the Trade Mark Act became law. Any piece bearing the words 'Trade Mark' therefore, can be assumed to date from 1862 onward.

Following the law relating to companies of limited liability, the word Limited or its abbreviations appears after 1860, though more commonly on pieces dating from 1885 onwards.

When a piece bears a pattern number of name, it can be assumed to date no earlier than about 1810.

Royal Arms incorporated into a mark indicates a date after 1800.

During the mid 19th century the word 'Royal' was commonly added to the Manufacturer's name or trade name and, consequently, pieces bearing this word can usually be placed after 1850.

HANDLES

| 1550 Tudor drop. | 1560 Early Stuart loop. | 1570 Early Stuart loop. | 1620 Early Stuart loop. | 1660 Stuart drop. | 1680 Stuart drop. | 1690 William & Mary solid backplate. | 1700 William & Mary split tail. |

| 1700 Queen Anne solid backplate. | 1705 Queen Anne ring. | 1710 Queen Anne loop. | 1720 Early Georgian pierced. | 1720 Early Georgian brass drop. | 1730 Cut away backplate. | 1740 Georgian plain brass loop. |

| 1750 Georgian shield drop. | 1755 French style. | 1760 Rococo style. | 1765 Chinese style. | 1770 Georgian ring. | 1780 Late Georgian stamped. | 1790 Late Georgian stamped. |

| 1810 Regency knob. | 1820 Regency lions mask. | 1825 Campaign. | 1840 Early Victorian porcelain. | 1850 Victorian reeded. | 1880 Porcelain or wood knob. | 1890 Late Victorian loop. | 1910 Art Nouveau. |

PEDIMENTS

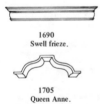  

| 1690 Swell frieze. | 1700 Queen Anne. | 1705 Double arch. |

| 1705 Queen Anne. | 1710 Triple arch. | 1715 Broken circular. |

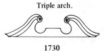

| 1720 Cavetto. | 1730 Swan neck. | 1740 Broken arch |

| 1740 Banner top. | 1750 Dentil cornice. | 1755 Fret cut. |

LEGS

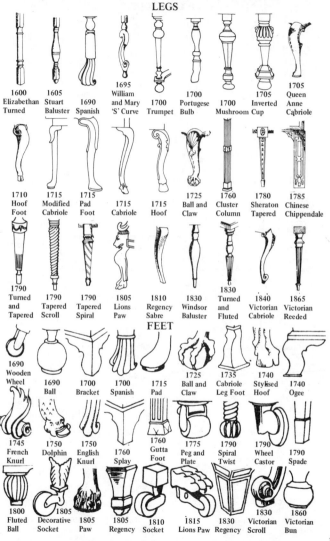

| 1600 Elizabethan Turned | 1605 Stuart Baluster | 1690 Spanish | 1695 William and Mary 'S' Curve | 1700 Trumpet | 1700 Portugese Bulb | 1700 Mushroom | 1705 Inverted Cup | 1705 Queen Anne Cabriole |

| 1710 Hoof Foot | 1715 Modified Cabriole | 1715 Pad Foot | 1715 Cabriole | 1715 Hoof | 1725 Ball and Claw | 1760 Cluster Column | 1780 Sheraton Tapered | 1785 Chinese Chippendale |

| 1790 Turned and Tapered | 1790 Tapered Scroll | 1790 Tapered Spiral | 1805 Lions Paw | 1810 Regency Sabre | 1830 Windsor Baluster | 1830 Turned and Fluted | 1840 Victorian Cabriole | 1865 Victorian Reeded |

FEET

| 1690 Wooden Wheel | 1690 Ball | 1700 Bracket | 1700 Spanish | 1715 Pad | 1725 Ball and Claw | 1735 Cabriole Leg Foot | 1740 Stylised Hoof | 1740 Ogee |

| 1745 French Knurl | 1750 Dolphin | 1750 English Knurl | 1760 Splay | 1760 Gutta Foot | 1775 Peg and Plate | 1790 Spiral Twist | 1790 Wheel Castor | 1790 Spade |

| 1800 Fluted Ball | 1805 Decorative Socket | 1805 Paw | 1805 Regency | 1810 Socket | 1815 Lions Paw | 1830 Regency | 1830 Victorian Scroll | 1860 Victorian Bun |

11

CHAIR BACKS

1660
Charles II.

1705
Queen Anne.

1745
Chippendale.

1745
Chippendale.

1750
Georgian.

1750
Hepplewhite.

1750
Chippendale.

1760
French Rococo.

1760
Gothic.

1760
Splat back.

1770
Chippendale
ladder back.

1785
Windsor
wheel back.

1785
Lancashire
spindle back.

1785
Lancashire
ladder back.

1790
Shield and
feathers.

1795
Shield back.

1795
Hepplewhite
camel back.

1795
Hepplewhite.

1810
Late Georgian
bar back.

1810
Thomas Hope
'X' frame.

1810
Regency
rope back.

1815
Regency
cane back.

1820
Regency.

1820
Empire.

1820
Regency
bar back.

1830
Regency
bar back.

1830
William IV
bar back.

1830
William IV.

1835
Lath back.

1840
Victorian
balloon back.

1845
Victorian.

1845
Victorian
bar back.

1850
Victorian.

1860
Victorian.

1870
Victorian.

1875
Cane back.

Mother-of-pearl in-laid rosewood baro-meter, circa 1850, 44¾in. high.

Inlaid mahogany stick barometer by Negrety, 1850, 44in. long.

Oak barometer and timepiece, 1880's, 44in. high.

Early 18th century walnut pillar baro-meter, 3ft.3in. high.

Victorian oak cased baro-meter.

BRONZE

Bronze figure of a jaguar, 22¼in. long, 1920's.

Gilt bronze group of three putti, 1850's, 10¾in. wide.

19th century Japanese bronze group.

Early 17th century Florentine bronze figure from the Susini workshop, 6¾in. high.

Splashed gilt bronze vase, Chinese, 18th century, 29.5cm. high.

Bronze figure of Icarus, by Alfred Gilbert, 48.5cm. high.

Mid 19th century bronze group by Charles Cum-berworth, 13½in. high.

Chiparus bronze and ivory figure of a dancing girl, 43.5cm. high, 1920's.

Bronze bust signed Macgillivray, 11¼in. high, dated 1915.

Bronze figure of a horse, circa 1880, 6in. wide.

19th century Japanese bronze, 4ft.4in. long.

Hagenauer bronze vase, circa 1910, 11.5cm. high.

13

CADDIES & BOXES

Regency penwork tea caddy, 9in. wide.

George III ivory and pewter tea caddy, 5in. high.

Commonwealth carved oak bible box, 1657, 2ft. wide.

George III oval satinwood tea caddy with hinged lid, 6in. wide.

Late 17th century four case inro, unsigned.

Lacquered work box with lift-up lid and four drawers.

Reco Capey carved ebony box and cover, 21cm. high.

Regency mother-of-pearl tea caddy of bow-fronted form, 8in. wide.

Mid 19th century artist's paintbox, 1ft.10in. wide, English.

One of a pair of George III mahogany and satinwood knife boxes, 22.5cm. wide.

English box and counters, 1755-1760, enamelled on copper, 6.5cm. wide.

Mahogany 'Duke of York' apothecary cabinet, circa 1780.

CAMERAS

Rare Johnson pantoscopic camera, circa 1860.

'The Telephot' ferrotype button camera, circa 1900, English.

Stirn's small waistcoat detective camera, in brass, second model, circa 1888.

Fine quarter-plate field camera by Sanderson.

German gold cane handle, 2½in. high, circa 1730.

English ivory pique cane handle, 4in. high, 1667.

French Art Nouveau cane handle, circa 1900.

Rhinoceros horn and silver pique cane handle, circa 1700, 12.5cm. long.

Late 19th century Meissen parasol handle, 4.3cm. high.

CARVED WOOD

Carved oak sternboard from the boat of an 18th century Dutch flagship, 33in. wide.

Balsa wood mask made for the 'Goelede' society, Yoruba tribe.

Mid 18th century South German carved wood group.

Early 17th century yew wood mortar, 6¼in. high.

Bas relief wood sculpture, by Norman Forrest, 1930's, 93cm. high.

Carved walnut figure group of two cavaliers, 41in. high.

Large Egyptian wood mummy mask.

Maori carved wooden house post, before 1840, 4ft.2½in. high.

Atelier Hagenauer patinated metal and carved wood head, 27cm. high, circa 1920.

Late 17th century figure of Putai, in lacquered wood, 22in. high.

17th century Spanish carved wood and painted polychrome religious group, 19in.

Lower Rhine oak relief, 19½in. high, circa 1500.

15

ALBARELLI

A Sicilian albarello, 20cm. high, 17th century.

Dated Tuscan albarello, 13.3cm. high, 1600.

ANSBACH

One of a pair of Ansbach equestrian figures, circa 1730, 24.5cm. high.

18th century Ansbach faience tankard, with pewter footrim, 1791, 24.5cm. high.

AUSTRIAN

Turn Art Nouveau ceramic dish, Austrian, circa 1900, 44cm. long.

An Austrian glazed earthenware jardiniere and stand, circa 1905.

BAYREUTH

Fine and rare Bayreuth Hausmaler bowl, 18.5cm. diam., circa 1740.

Bayreuth Hausmaler teabowl and saucer, circa 1740.

BELLARMINE

Antique brown glazed stoneware bellarmine jug, 13in. high.

Early 17th century Frenchen stoneware bellarmine jug, 25cm. high.

BELLEEK

Belleek tea kettle on stand.

One of a pair of Belleek pitchers with scrolled handles and applied floral decoration.

BERLIN

One of a pair of Berlin porcelain cabinet cups and saucers with gilt decoration.

One of a pair of Berlin covered chocolate pots, 7¾in. and 5½in. high, circa 1830.

BOTTGER

Rare Bottger doublehandled beaker and saucer, circa 1720-25.

Very rare Bottger jug and cover, circa 1720.

BOULOGNE

Boulogne glazed pottery figure, 47.5cm. high, 1925.

Boulogne crackle glazed pottery figure, 61cm. high, 1920's.

BRISTOL

Bristol made cider mug, 1842, 5in. high.

Rare Bristol figure of a goatherder, 10¾in. high, about 1775.

BURMANTOFT

Burmantoft vase, about 1885, painted by 'L.K', 8½in. high.

Burmantofts jardiniere and stand, 50½in. high.

CARDEW, MICHAEL

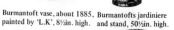

Michael Cardew stoneware bowl with tapering foot rim, 1960's, 7¾in. diam.

Michael Cardew large slipware dish, circa 1930, 16½in. diam.

BOW

Rare Bow figure of a goldfinch, 3¼in. high, circa 1758-62.

BRITISH

Victorian jug and basin set.

CAPODIMONTE

Capodimonte tureen, circa 1750, 11in. diam.

CASTEL DURANTE

Castel Durante dated wet drug jar, 1644, 22.5cm. high.

CHINA

Pair of Bow figures of a gallant and lady, 6in. high, about 1760.

Victorian brown glazed pottery cheese dish.

Extremely rare Capodimonte Commedia Dell'Arte group of the Harlequin and two other figures, by Guiseppe Gricci, dated around 1750.

Mid 17th century Castel Durante bottle, 22.5cm. high.

CASTELLI

Late 18th century Castelli plaque, 26.8cm. long.

18th century Castelli plate, 24.2cm. diam.

CAUGHLEY

A Caughley cylindrical mug printed in blue, 6in. high, circa 1780.

Caughley teabowl and saucer painted in underglaze blue, circa 1785.

CHAMPIONS BRISTOL

Fine Champions Bristol bell-shaped mug, 5in. high, about 1775.

One of a set of four Champions Bristol figures of the Elements, 10in. to 11¼in. high.

CHANTILLY

Chantilly two-handled bowl, 11in. wide.

Chantilly figure of a Chinese man, 7in. high.

CHELSEA

Chelsea candlestick group of birds, circa 1762, 7in. high.

Attractive Chelsea fluted teabowl and saucer painted in Kakiemon palette, 1749-52.

Chelsea white figure of a musician, 8in. high, about 1755.

Fine Chelsea Hans Sloane botanical plate.

CLARICE CLIFF

Attractive Clarice Cliff 'bizarre' teapot and cream jug, 1930's.

Clarice Cliff 'bizarre' vase, 21cm. high, 1930's.

COALBROOKDALE

Coalbrookdale pot pourri vase, cover and stand, 6¾in. high.

One of a pair of Coalbrookdale baluster vases, 10in. high.,

COALPORT

A scarce Coalport cup and saucer with 'bleu de roi' ground.

Coalport flower-encrusted ewer, 10¼in. high, circa 1830.

A Coalport plate from an attractive set of twenty-four, each painted with a scene of game birds, by P. Simpson, signed, 9in.

Henrietta, circa 1750, china figure by Coalport, 7in. high.

COMMEMORATIVE

Commemorative mug, 1838, made for Victoria's coronation, 3¾in. high.

A rare commemorative Bragget pot of large size, possibly by Ralph Simpson, circa 1700, 7¼in. high.

COPELAND

Copeland Edward VII memorial vase, 1910, 7in. high.

Copeland Parian figure of Sir Walter Scott, circa 1860, 11¾in. high.

COPELAND & GARRETT

One of a pair of Copeland & Garrett New Stone plates, 21.5cm. diam.

Copeland & Garrett figure of Narcissus by John Gibson, 1846, 31cm. high.

COPELAND SPODE

Copeland Spode tureens and dish, circa 1850.

Part of a Copeland Spode seventeen-piece dessert service.

COPER, HANS

Hans Coper spherical stoneware vase, 1960's, 8½in. high.

A stoneware vase, by Hans Coper, the flattened bowl with slightly swelling sides, 16cm. high.

DAVENPORT

Davenport cup and saucer, circa 1870.

Part of a Davenport tea and coffee service, circa 1870, sixty-one pieces.

19

DECK, THEODORE

Late 19th century Theodore Deck duck, 12in. high.

Theodore deck faience dish, circa 1870, 14¼in. diam.

DELFT

Rare delft mug, mid 18th century, 4½in. high.

Late 18th century delft dish, 13in. diam.

DELFT, BRISTOL

Bristol delft blue and white two-handled jar, 6¼in. high.

Bristol delft polychrome blue dash portrait charger, circa 1710, 34cm. diam.

DELFT, DUTCH

Fine Dutch Delft tea kettle and cover, 25cm. high.

Dutch Delft bottle, early 18th century, 22.2cm. high.

DELFT, ENGLISH

English delft dry drug jar, 7in. high.

Small English delftware cistern and cover, 1644, 14in. high, probably by Christian Wilhelm.

DELFT, IRISH

Rare Irish delft plate, 9¾in., about 1760.

One of a pair of rare Dublin delft vases, late 18th century, 3¾in. high.

DELFT, LAMBETH

Early 18th century Lambeth delft globular jar, 5¼in. diam.

Mid 18th century Lambeth polychrome delft plate, 33.3cm. diam.

DELFT, LIVERPOOL

Very rare late 18th century Liverpool delft leaf dish, 5½in. high.

Liverpool delft jug, circa 1760-70, 7¾in. high.

20

DELFT, LONDON

DE MORGAN

Late 17th century London delft fuddling cup, 3¼in. high.

Late 17th century London delft posset pot and cover, 5¾in. high.

William De Morgan lustre bottle vase, 17cm. high.

William De Morgan lustre saucer dish, Fulham period, 36cm. diam.

DERBY

Derby figure of a spaniel, circa 1765, 8cm. long.

Pair of Derby 'mansion house' dwarfs, 6¾in. high, about 1820.

Fine Derby bell-shaped mug, 4in. high, about 1760.

Rare Derby figure of a monkey playing the double-bass, 5in. high.

DERBY, BLOOR

DERBY, ROYAL CROWN

One of a pair of Bloor Derby sauce tureens, covers and stands, 8½in. wide.

Bloor Derby figure of a lady seated in a chair, 5½in. high.

Part of a forty-piece Royal Crown Derby tea service, dated for 1898.

Royal Crown Derby slender two-handled oviform vase and cover, 14½in. high.

DOCCIA

DOULTON, ROYAL

One of a pair of Doccia blue and white moutardieres, 11.5cm. high, circa 1760.

Rare Doccia bust of the Roman Emperor Augustus, 1750-60, 51cm. high.

One of a pair of Royal Doulton vases, by Emma Shute, 21cm. high.

Royal Doulton jug of a Regency beau.

DOULTON

Doulton silver mounted stoneware tyg, 6¼in. high, circa 1900.

Unusual Doulton 'Dickens' jug, after a design by Noke, 10½in. high, circa 1936.

Doulton saltglazed figure of Queen Victoria, 11½in. high, circa 1902.

Doulton stoneware teapot, 6¾in. high, dated 1878, with silver lid.

DRESDEN

Part of an early 20th century Dresden coffee service of forty-three pieces.

A large pair of Dresden figures of a gentleman playing bagpipes and his companion with a hurdy-gurdy, 47cm. high.

DUTCH

Early 18th century Dutch tin glazed bird cage, 39cm. high.

Large Tournai dish decorated at The Hague, circa 1780, 40cm. diam.

EARTHENWARE

Red earthenware globular flagon, probably West African, 20cm. high.

One of a pair of unusual earthenware vases, circa 1880, 36.8cm. high, on jardiniere style stands.

EUROPEAN

Swiss tin glazed chest of drawers, 17.5cm. high.

Saintonage oval dish, 17th century, 31cm. long.

FAENZA

Italian Faenza dish, dated 1537, 47cm. diam.

Early 16th century Faenza drug jar, 22.5cm. high, restored.

FRANKENTHAL

Frankenthal coffee pot, circa 1760, 10¼in. high.

A Frankenthal figure of a fruit seller, 14cm. high, 1759-62.

22

FRENCH

Mid 17th century Nevers double-handled urn, 33cm. high.

French biscuit porcelain and gilt metal casket, 3½in. diameter, circa 1900.

FULHAM

Mid 18th century Fulham stoneware mug with foliage encrusted decoration.

CHINA

Rare Fulham stoneware posset pot, 17th century, 6¾in. high.

GERMAN

German faience Hanau blue and white two-handled octagonal jardiniere.

South German faience pewter mounted tankard, circa 1744, 20cm. high.

GOSS

A fine and rare Goss model of a polar bear.

Early 20th century Goss model of John Knox's House, 4in. high.

HOCHST

Hochst teapot and cover, circa 1765-70, 10.2cm. high.

Hochst tea caddy and cover possibly painted by Heinrich Usinger, circa 1770, 14cm. high.

ITALIAN

Late 18th century Italian group, 18.5cm. high.

Late 18th century Marcolini part coffee service.

JONES, GEORGE

Small, late Victorian pottery butter dish by George Jones.

Good 'majolica' camel vase, probably George Jones, circa 1870, 9½in. high.

BERNARD LEACH

Bernard Leach stoneware bottle vase, 1960's, 7¾in. high.

Bernard Leach stoneware 'Pilgrim' dish, 1960's, 12½in. diam.

LEEDS

Leeds creamware ship-decorated plate, circa 1800-1820. 9¾in. diam.

A figure of a Leeds pearlware stallion, 16¼in. high, circa 1790.

LIMOGES

Pair of octagonal based Limoges candlesticks, 6¾in. high.

Limoges enamelled pot and cover, 1920's, 11.5cm., by Sarlandie.

LIVERPOOL

Liverpool blue and white shell-shaped pickle dish, 4¼in. wide.

Liverpool blue and white pear-shaped coffee pot, 8½in. high.

LONGTON HALL

Longton Hall leaf-shaped bowl, 3in. diam., about 1755.

One of a pair of Longton Hall figures of seated nuns, chipped, circa 1775.

LOWESTOFT

Lowestoft jug with kick-back handle and pink border, 3¼in. high, circa 1785.

Lowestoft porcelain figures of musicians, circa 1780-90, 17.8cm. high.

LUDWIGSBURG

Late 19th century Ludwigsburg group of figures, 25.5cm. high.

Ludwigsburg group of a river god, circa 1770, 20cm. wide.

LUSTRE

Rare pink lustre jug, 13cm. high, circa 1800-1810.

Good Clement lustre charger, circa 1900, 48cm. diam.

MACINTYRES

Unusual Moorcroft Macintyre jardiniere, circa 1900, 7in. high.

Florian vase made at Macintyres, circa 1893.

24

MAJOLICA

Large late 19th century majolica jardiniere with a stand.

One of a pair of majolica ewer jugs, 19in. high.

MARSEILLE

A fine Marseilles faience plate, with fish and lobster design.

CHINA

A Marseilles faience two-handled tureen and cover painted in colours with bouquets of flowers, 36cm. wide.

MARTINWARE

Martin Brothers jardiniere, 7¼in. high, dated 11-1900, incised signature

Martin Brothers bird, 9¾in. high, incised signature, dated 7-1892.

MASON'S

Large Mason's ironstone blue and white platter, circa 1820.

Impressive Mason's porcelain vase, circa 1810, 25½in. high, small repair.

MEISSEN

Early Meissen bowl and cover, 10cm. high, circa 1730.

Meissen group modelled by J. J. Kaendler, 1744, 8½in. high.

Meissen milk jug, in the manner of C. F. Herold.

A large late 19th century Meissen group of Count Bruth's tailor, 43cm. high.

MENNECY

Rare Mennecy snuff box in white, mid 18th century, 4.5cm. high.

Mid 18th century Mennecy pomade pot and cover, 8.6cm. high.

METTLACH

One of a pair of German Mettlach jardinieres, 23in. wide, signed Warth.

Mettlach vase, circa 1900-10, 40cm. high.

MINTON

Mid 19th century Minton majolica teapot, 5in. high.

Minton porcelain plaque, circa 1870, 37cm. high.

Minton reticulated teacup and saucer, impressed marks.

One of a pair of Minton pate-sur-pate vases, 7in. high.

MOORCROFT

Moorcroft vase in 'Moonlit Blue' Hazeldene pattern, 9¼in. high, 1920-30.

Part of an eleven-piece Moorcroft coffee service in Hazeldene pattern.

Rare Moorcroft Florian-ware vase, dated 1899, 16in. high.

Moorcroft bowl, 9in. diam., circa 1901-13.

MOTTO WARE

A Dartmouth pottery jug, inscribed 'No road is long with Good Company'.

An Aller Vale pottery hat-pin stand, decorated with ship design.

MURRAY, WILLIAM

A stoneware oviform vase, by Wm. Staite Murray, 21.5cm. high.

A stoneware flared bowl, by Wm. Staite Murray, 21cm. diam.

NANTGARW

Nantgarw deep dish, 10¼in. diam., 1817-20.

Rare Nantgarw pedestal dish, 5¾in. high, 1817-20.

NAPLES

19th century white porcelain Naples figure, 10¾in. high, signed.

One of two Naples armorial wet drug jars, 1690, 22cm. high.

NEWHALL

Part of a Newhall tea service, twenty-eight pieces, 1795-1805.

Newhall jug, circa 1787.

NIDERVILLE

One of a set of four Niderville figures of Summer and Autumn, 13cm. high.

CHINA

One of a rare pair of Niderville covered vases, 15¼in. high, circa 1780.

NOVE

Majolica dish made at Nove da Bassano, circa 1770, 15½in. diam.

A finely modelled Le Nove figure group.

NYMPHENBURG

Porcelain ice-bucket from the Nymphenburg factory, 6½in. high.

Nymphenburg model of a parrot, circa 1850-62, 18.7cm. high.

PARIAN

Samuel Alcock & Co. figure of the Duke of Wellington, 11in. high, circa 1852.

Robinson & Leadbetter coloured Parian figure, 12¼in. high, circa 1890.

PARIS

Paris raspberry ground cache-pot, circa 1870, 18.5cm. high.

Pair of 19th century Paris porcelain figures, 24½in. high.

PETIT, JACOB

One of a pair of Jacob Petit vases, circa 1860.

One of a pair of Jacob Petit urn-shaped porcelain wine coolers, 12in. high.

PILKINGTON

Unusual Pilkington Royal Lancastrian plate, 12¾in. diam., dated for 1906.

Small Pilkington Royal Lancastrian ovoid jar and cover, 1926, 12cm. high.

PLYMOUTH

Pair of Plymouth figures depicting a gardener and his companion, 1768-71.

Rare Plymouth teapot and cover, 6¼in. high, about 1768-70.

POOLE

Carter, Stabler & Adams Poole pottery vase, circa 1930, 9¾in. high.

Poole pottery fish glazed in green with a black base, 17in. high.

POTSCHAPPEL

Potschappel porcelain fruit basket on stand, circa 1860.

A pair of Dresden vases, by Carl Thierne of Potschappel, 22½in. high.

PRATTWARE

A Prattware tea caddy depicting George III, 6¼in. high, 1780-90.

Rare Prattware Toby jug, circa 1780-90, 10in. high.

RIDGWAY

Large Ridgway parian group of Venus and Cupid, 1858, 18¾in. high.

Part of a twenty-one piece dessert service, circa 1825-35.

RIE, LUCY

A porcelain bowl, by Lucie Rie, of wide conical form, 23.5cm. diam.

A stoneware vase by Lucie Rie, covered in cream grey glaze, 30cm. high.

ROCKINGHAM

One of a pair of Rockingham plates, 9in. diam.

Unusually plain Rockingham swan.

ROMAN

Early 19th century circular Roman mosaic plaque, 7.3cm. diam.

Roman mosaic plaque, circa 1825, 3¼in. wide.

28

ROSENTHAL

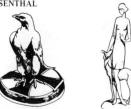

Interesting old Imperial German porcelain desk ornament, by Rosenthal, Bavaria, 7½in. high.

Rosenthal porcelain group of a young woman and a fawn, 34cm. high, 1930's.

ROYAL COPENHAGEN

A Royal Copenhagen porcelain vase of double gourd shape, 21cm. high.

CHINA

A Royal Copenhagen group of St. Paul slaying the Lie, circa 1925, 24½in. high.

ROYAL DUX

Royal Dux group of a peasant and a bull, circa 1910, 33cm. wide.

Large pair of Royal Dux figures of a Shepherdess and Shepherd, 79cm. high.

ROZENBURG

Small Rozenburg vase, circa 1900, 11cm. high.

Rozenburg pottery vase with twin loop handles, circa 1900, 26.5cm. high.

RUSKIN

Ruskin high-fired vase, 8in. high, dated 1924.

Ruskin high-fired bowl, 4in., dated 1915.

SALTGLAZE

Rare small saltglaze bear mug, 3½in. high, about 1740.

Coloured saltglaze cream jug, 3in. high, about 1760.

SAMSON

A Samson two-handled oval tureen with domed cover, 37cm. wide.

Pair of Samson parrots on tree-stumps, repaired, 42cm. high.

Samson group of the Levee du Roi of five figures, 38cm. wide.

A Samson pear-shaped coffee pot with domed cover, 21cm. tall.

29

SAVONA

Late 17th century Savona drug jar and cover, 34cm. high.

Early 17th century Savona tazza, 25.5cm. diam.

SEVRES

A Sevres cabinet plate painted by D. Ceniers, late 19th century, 24cm. diam.

An unusual 18th century Sevres bleu du roi ewer, 25.2cm. high.

SITZENDORF

Sitzendorf table centre-piece with pierced basket, 29cm. high.

Late 19th century Sitzendorf clockcase, 38cm. high.

SLIPWARE

Staffordshire slipware baking dish, freely decorated with a netting pattern.

Slipware baking dish with typical notched rim.

SPODE

Spode cup and saucer, pattern 967, circa 1810.

Spode pink ground oviform vase with loop handles, circa 1820, 18.5cm. high.

Part of a ninety-piece Spode 'New Stone' dinner and dessert service, early 19th century.

Spode pastille burner and cover, circa 1830, 4in. high.

STAFFORDSHIRE

Staffordshire jug with pictorial decoration.

Staffordshire portrait bust of George Washington, 21cm. high.

White Staffordshire salt-glazed teapot and cover, 4¾in. high, about 1740.

Staffordshire figure of Sir Robert Peel, circa 1850, 12¼in. high.

STONEWARE

19th century stoneware quart jug with embossed scenic decoration.

Quimper Art Deco decorated stoneware vase, 1920's, 18cm. high.

SUNDERLAND

Sunderland lustre jug, circa 1840, 7¼in. high.

CHINA

Mid 19th century Sunderland lustre frog mug.

SWANSEA

Swansea tea cup and saucer.

Swansea plate painted with a view of Pembroke Castle.

TERRACOTTA

Late 18th century French terracotta group, 15½in. high.

Italian polychrome terracotta bust of Pope Leo X, early 16th century, 37.5cm. high.

TURNER

Large Turner biscuit jug, circa 1800, 8¼in. high.

Turner blue and white jasper rectangular plaque, 8 x 5½in.

URBINO

Urbino majolica dish showing the story of Pluto and Proserpine, circa 1530, 12in. diam.

Urbino 'Istoriato' dish, 25.5cm. diam., circa 1537, painted by Francesco Xanto Avelli.

VENETIAN

16th century Venetian wet drug jar, 20cm. high.

Early 16th century 'majolica' vase, Venetian.

VIENNA

Viennese porcelain tankard with ormolu thumb-grip and cover-lift.

Late 19th century Vienna decorated Eaas and Czjzcr Schlaggenwald plaque, 50.3cm. diam.

VINCENNES

VOLKSTEDT

Vincennes porcelain covered supper dish, circa 1755, 8¼in. wide.

Vincennes white chinoiserie group, circa 1745, 19in. wide.

Pair of Volkstedt figures of a Gallant and his Companion, circa 1900, 41cm. high.

Late 19th century Eckert & Co. Volkstedt group, 22cm. high.

VYSE, CHARLES

WALFORD, JAMES

Stoneware foliate bowl, by Charles Vyse, 7¼in. diam.

Charles Vyse figure of 'Barnet Fair', circa 1933, 10¼in. high.

20th century James Walford stoneware model of a head of a shoebill, 7¼in. high.

20th century James Walford stoneware model of an hippopotamus head, 6¾in. wide.

WEDGWOOD

Wedgwood creamware cylindrical mug, circa 1765, 12cm. high, transfer-printed in black.

19th century Wedgwood blue jasperware circular jardiniere, 9½in. diam.

Wedgwood 'Rosso Antico' D-shaped bulb pot and cover, 7¼in. wide.

One of a pair of Wedgwood candlesticks modelled as dolphins, late 18th century, 10in. high.

WEMYSS

WESTERWALD

Part of a Robert Heron & Son Wemyssware toilet set, 20th century.

Wemyssware moulded jug, circa 1910, 8in. high.

Early 18th century Westerwald saltglaze stoneware jug, 25cm. high.

Early 18th century Westerwald salt cellar with saltglaze, 17cm. high.

Whieldon green glazed rectangular tea caddy, circa 1760, 11.5cm. high.

Whieldon cow creamer and cover, circa 1760, 5¼in. high.

Whieldon type Toby jug, circa 1750, 6¼in. high.

Wedgwood-Whieldon teapot and cover moulded with fruits and foliage, circa 1760-65, 5¼in. high.

WOOD, ENOCH

Massive Enoch Wood pearlware jug, late 18th century, 17in. high.

Rare Enoch Wood figure of John Liston, 6¼in. high, about 1820.

WOOD, RALPH

Ralph Wood elephant spill vase, circa 1770-80, 8in. high.

An inscribed and dated Ralph Wood jug of large size, modelled by Jean Voyez, 9½in. high, 1788.

WORCESTER

Worcester straight-sided mug with transfer-printed border, circa 1770.

Worcester 'Beckoning Chinaman' teapot and cover, 6in. high, about 1755-58.

Early Worcester sweetmeat dish, 3in. high, about 1752-54.

Worcester coffee pot and cover, 23.5cm. high.

Worcester First period cylindrical mustard pot with flower finial, 4in. high.

, A Worcester fluted coffee cup and saucer, 1765-70.

Large Worcester hexagonal vase and cover, decorated in Imari palette, 26in. high.

An early Worcester cream jug with a Long Eliza figure, 3¼in. high, 1753-55.

33

WORCESTER, CHAMBERLAIN

WORCESTER, DR. WALL

Chamberlain Worcester card tray with painted centre.

Chamberlain Worcester vase and cover of baluster shape, 46cm. high.

A Dr. Wall period hot water jug complete with cover.

Dr. Wall Worcester teapot, 6in. high, with scale blue base.

WORCESTER, FLIGHT, BARR & BARR

WORCESTER, GRAINGERS

19th century Barr, Flight & Barr soup tureen, cover and stand from a dinner service of forty-two pieces.

One of a pair of Flight, Barr & Barr claret ground plates, circa 1820, 22.5cm. diam.

One of a pair of Grainger sauce tureens, circa 1810.

One of a garniture of three Grainger Worcester pot pourri vases, circa 1815, 13½in. and 10¾in. high.

WORCESTER, ROYAL

WROTHAM

Royal Worcester vase and cover, 1899.

Royal Worcester plate, dated for 1912, 9in. diam.

Wrotham pottery jug, by George Richardson, 6½in. high.

Wrotham slipware inscribed and dated tyg, by Henry Ifield, 13cm. high, 1644.

YORKSHIRE

ZURICH

A rare Yorkshire equestrian figure, 8¾in. high, circa 1780.

Late 18th century Yorkshire 'squat' Toby jug, with caryatid handle, 7¾in. high.

Mid 18th century Zurich plate, 23cm. diam.

Zurich porcelain figure representing Painting, 6½in. high.

ARITA

Fine 18th century Arita blue and white hexagonal lobed bowl with floral design, Fuku mark, 21.2cm. diam.

17th century Japanese Arita blue and white lidded porcelain jar, 13in. high.

BLUE & WHITE

Mid 19th century Japanese blue and white porcelain dish, 14½in. diam.

ORIENTAL CHINA

Mid 17th century Chinese blue and white porcelain vase, 8¼in. high.

CANTON

Canton dish, typically painted and gilt, 35cm. diam., circa 1870.

One of a pair of Canton famille rose vases, mid 19th century, 35cm. high.

CHENGHUA

Chinese porcelain jar of the Chenghua period, decorated in underglaze blue, 10.3cm.

Doucai wine cup decorated in blue, red, yellow and pale green, with six character mark of Chenghua.

CHINESE

Chinese white porcelain ewer of the Liao dynasty with a simulated cane work handle.

Chinese Jizhou teabowl with brown glaze, 11.5cm. diam.

Sui dynasty straw glazed equestrian tomb figure, 13in. high.

One of a pair of apple-green Chinese porcelain vases, 13¾in. high.

DAOGUANG

Small, Daoguang period, famille rose ruby ground bowl with floral decoration and scenic views in panels.

Chinese porcelain orchid vase of the Daoguang period.

EDO

Early Edo period seto chaire with ivory cover, 5.5cm. high

Early Edo period pottery chaire with ivory cover, 7cm. high.

35

EXPORTWARE

18th century Chinese export porcelain documentary punchbowl.

Oriental export porcelain chocolate pot, late 18th century, 10in. high.

FAMILLE NOIRE

Mid 19th century famille noire vase with waisted neck, 53.5cm. high.

One of a pair of large Chinese famille noire pear-shaped vases painted with dignitaries and immortals, 21¾in. high.

FAMILLE ROSE

One of a pair of mid 19th century Chinese famille rose jars and covers.

Famille rose porcelain plate, 8¾in. diam., decorated with blossom, insects and plants, late 18th century.

FAMILLE VERTE

One of a pair of famille verte brushwashers and water droppers.

Pair of famille verte Immortals, 18½in. high.

FUKAGAWA

One of a pair of løbed Fukagawa bowls, circa 1900, 10¼in. long.

Fukagawa bowl, circa 1900, with incurved rim, 15½in. high.

GUAN

Guan compressed jar with crackleware glaze, 4¼in. high.

18th century Guan type vase, 6in. high.

HAMADA

A stoneware circular dish, by Shoji Hamada, 32cm. diam.

A stoneware flared vase, by Shoji Hamada, 19.5cm. high.

HAN

Rare green glazed model of a stove of the Han dynasty.

Unglazed pottery head from the Han dynasty, 4in. high.

HICHOZAN

Late 19th century Hichozan Shinpo vase, 49.5cm. high, with pierced neck.

One of a pair of Hichozan Shinpo vases, circa 1870, 17in. high.

HOZAN

Late 19th century Hozan Satsuma dish with fluted rim, 10in. diam.

ORIENTAL CHINA

One of a pair of Hozan earthenware vases, circa 1900, 6¼in. high.

IMARI

Imari porcelain goldfish bowl with floral decoration, 20in. diam.

Fine Japanese Imari charger, 23½in. diam.

Japanese Imari vase from the late 19th century, 62cm. high.

Late 17th century green ground Imari wine ewer, 15.5cm. high.

JAPANESE

Japanese whisky set with five bowls.

Japanese plique a jour vase with gold wire framed enamel decoration.

KAKIEMON

Late 17th century Kakiemon wine-pot and cover of ovoid form.

A fine teabowl and saucer painted in the Kakiemon palette, circa 1770.

KANGXI

Kangxi famille verte porcelain plate, 23cm. diam.

One of a pair of Kangxi period famille verte Buddhistic lion joss stick holders, 20.5cm. high.

Kangxi rare underglaze blue and red jardiniere, 8¾in. diam.

Kangxi blue and white stem cup, 5½in. high.

KINKOZAN

Japanese Kinkozan bowl with wavy rim, circa 1870.

Kinkozan earthenware vase, 17in. high, circa 1870.

KUTANI

Japanese Kutani plate decorated with birds and foliage, 14in. diam.

A Kutani vase and cover, a young sake tester modelled on one side, 27cm. high, late 18th century.

MING

Chinese wine ewer made in the 14th century and painted in copper red, 12¾in. high.

16th century Ming jar in blue and white porcelain, 15in. diam.

MISCELLANEOUS

Mid 16th century Isnik pottery stemmed dish, 12in. diam.

Ban Chiang grey pottery jar with globular body and flared neck, 2nd/1st millenium B.C., 12in. high.

KOREAN

12th century Korean celadon wine ewer, 7in. high.

Korean Yi dynasty blue and white globular jar, cracked, 8½in. diam.

LANG YAO

18th century Lang Yao bottle, 11¼in. high.

Early 18th century Lang Yao baluster vase, 14in. high.

Unusual Ming dynasty celadon group, 9in. high.

Early Ming blue and white porcelain flask, 10in. high.

16th century Annamese saucer dish, painted with underglaze blue.

Rare Namban figure of a bishop carrying a crozier and rosary, 12in. tall.

38

NANKIN

One of a pair of Nankin style blue and white porcelain vases, 10¾in. high.

Nankin tureen, decorated in polychrome with Oriental garden scenes and with a domed cover.

PERSIAN

18th century Persian blue and white baluster scent bottle, 7½in. high.

ORIENTAL CHINA

Persian dish 12th/13th century, made in Rayy, 9½in. diam.

QIANLONG

Qianlong blue and white charger decorated with a hunting scene, 17in. diam.

Qianlong period blue and white pilgrim vase, 51cm. high.

Qianlong incense burner and cover surmounted with a Dog of Fo.

One of a pair of mid 19th century Qianlong blue and white vases, 49.5cm. high.

QING

Celadon vase with central floral panel, circa 1870.

Chinese porcelain cockerel, circa 1800.

RYOZAN

A Ryozan earthenware dish enamelled and gilt with child acrobats, 15.5cm. high, circa 1900.

Late 19th century Unzan Ryozan vase, 12in. high.

SATSUMA

19th century Satsuma decorated teapot, 7½in. high.

One of a pair of Satsuma baluster vases decorated with heads, 24cm. high.

Late 19th century Satsuma pottery vase decorated with figures, 8½in. high.

Outstanding Japanese Satsuma bowl with a gilt encrusted pictorial scene of the arrival of Chinese envoys, dated 1804.

SONG

Chinese white glazed jar from the Song dynasty, 10.5cm. high.

Song dynasty jar decorated with three stylised leaf sprays, 5¼in. high.

TANG

Tang dynasty dark green globular storage jar, 7¼in. high.

A Tang dynasty figure of a horse, 28in. wide.

WANLI

Wanli blue and white saucer dish, 15in. diam.

Wanli blue and white pear-shaped bottle, 27cm. high.

WEI

Wei dynasty unglazed pottery hound, 6½in. wide.

Wei dynasty grey pottery tomb attendant, 16in. high.

WUCAI

Fine Wucai baluster vase and cover, circa 1650-70, 14in. high.

Wucai transitional period jar, circa 1650, 10½in. high.

YIXING

Rare Chinese export Yixing figure, 19th century.

18th century Yixing teapot and cover.

YONGZHENG

One of a pair of Yongzheng famille rose fish bowls.

One of a pair of Yongzheng famille rose dishes, 12½in. diam.

YUAN

Yuan dynasty celadon incense burner, 3¾in. wide.

Rare 14th century Yuan dynasty stem cup stand, 7½in. diam.

19th century bracket clock, 14in. high, in mahogany and brass case.

Quarter repeating oak bracket clock, circa 1900, 16in. high.

Late 18th century mahogany quarter repeating bracket clock by William Dutton, 14in. high.

Eight-day English fusee bracket clock in ebony case by A. Quiguer, London, circa 1687.

Walnut striking bracket clock by Robt. Sadler, London, 14½in. high.

Japanned quarter repeating bracket timepiece, 13½in. high.

A Japanese striking bracket clock, 170mm. high.

Late 18th century musical bracket clock by Robert Ward, London, 61cm. high.

Mid 17th century bracket clock in an ebony veneered case by Pieter Visbagh, 10in. high.

Bracket clock by Thos. Tompion, London, circa 1700, 40cm. high.

George III mahogany bracket clock by Richard Webster, London, 18½in. high.

George III mahogany bracket clock by William Cozens of London, 1ft. 3½in. tall.

George III mahogany bracket clock by John Robert & Silva, London, 2ft.2in. high.

Dutch ebony gilt mounted bracket clock, 17in. high.

Walnut bracket clock by Daniel Quare, London, 14in. high.

Regency mahogany striking bracket clock by Panchaud & Cumming, London, 16in. high.

41

CARRIAGE CLOCKS

19th century carriage clock in the Japanese manner, 6¾in. high.

Porcelain mounted carriage clock, 6½in. high.

Late 19th century carriage clock by Nicole Nielson & Co., in silver case, 11.5cm. high.

Clock attributed to Mucha, circa 1900, 9in. high.

French brass striking carriage clock by Maurice & Co., 6½in. high.

Gilt spelter carriage clock, circa 1890, 6½in. high.

Gilt metal oval brass striking carriage clock by Drocourt, 5½in. high.

Grande sonnerie striking carriage clock by Drocourt, Paris.

French brass cased grande sonnerie carriage clock, 7in. high.

Early French gilt metal pendule de voyage, dial signed Dubois, Paris, circa 1780, 7½in. high.

French miniature carriage clock, 3¼in. high, with silvered dial.

English gilt metal carriage timepiece by Viner & Co., London, 4½in. high.

French gilt metal carriage clock, 8½in. high.

19th century petite sonnerie carriage clock by Joseph Berrolla, Paris.

Enamel mounted carriage clock in leather case, 6½in. high.

Elaborate gilt metal striking carriage clock, 8¼in. high.

42

Gilt spelter clock garniture, circa 1880, clock 14in. high.

Victorian china clock set with transfer decoration.

Gilt bronze clock garniture, clock in the form of an owl, circa 1890.

Gilt bronze and Dresden porcelain clock garniture, circa 1880, clock 14in. high.

Gilt bronze and Sevres clock garniture, circa 1880.

19th century French style clock garniture.

Late 19th century painted spelter and onyx clock garniture.

Ormolu and marble clock garniture, circa 1900, dial signed Camerden and Foster, New York, Made in France.

43

Small George III mahogany regulator, 6ft.11in. high.

Regency longcase clock with brass dial by N. Barwise, London.

A painted mahogany musical calendar longcase clock, 8ft. 10in. high.

Scottish longcase clock by David Greig, Perth, with shaped case.

French provincial longcase clock with elaborate brass pendulum.

Stylish modernistic clock, 1930's, 112cm. high.

Early 19th century mahogany longcase clock, 94in. high.

Wickerwork longcase clock.

Wrought iron longcase clock, circa 1920, 65½in. high.

Mahogany longcase clock, circa 1830, 93in. high.

Small longcase clock in a walnut marquetry case by J. Wise, circa 1680, 6ft.8in. high.

Mahogany longcase clock by Jn. and Wm. Mitchell, Glasgow, mid 19th century, 83in. high.

Early 19th century longcase clock signed Robin aux Galeries du Louvre, 6ft.10in. high.

Large marquetry chiming clock, circa 1900, 105½in. high.

Longcase clock in oak case, circa 1800.

19th century country-made lantern clock, 14in. high.

Provincial lantern clock by E. Bilbie, circa 1675, 10in. high.

Wing alarm lantern clock, 1ft.3in. high.

Small brass lantern time-piece with alarm, circa 1700, 170mm. high.

Lantern clock, circa 1690, by Joseph Windmills, London, 16in. high.

Louis XV provincial wall timepiece, 14½in. high.

Small lantern clock signed Sam Wichell, Piccadilly, 9in. high.

Balance wheel lantern clock by Baker, complete with doors.

Miniature travelling verge lantern clock by Charles Groode, London.

Alarm lantern clock by Wm. Kipling, London, 1ft.3in. high.

17th century brass lantern clock with one hand.

Small lantern clock, signed Robert Dingley, London, 9in. high.

English brass quarter strik-ing lantern clock, 12¾in. high.

Lantern clock by John Knibb, Oxford, circa 1690, 17½in. high.

Late 17th century brass lantern clock.

18th century Japanese lantern clock, 280mm. high.

45

Lalique frosted glass clock, 16cm. high, circa 1920.

Early 18th century gilt metal astronomical travelling clock by Wm. Winrowe, 10in. high.

German gilt metal striking table clock, 12.5cm. square.

Gilt metal and marble mantel clock, circa 1880, 13in. high.

19th century Dutch Delft clock with brass works, 18½in. high.

Art Deco bronze and marble mantel clock, 26cm. wide, 1920's.

Mid Victorian mantelpiece clock in brass and bronze mounted case.

Louis XVI white marble and ormolu timepiece, enamel dial signed Schmit a Paris, 1ft.3in. high.

Late 18th century Flemish painted mantel clock, 2ft. 4in. high.

Mid 19th century bronze and marble mantel clock, 21½in. high.

Black Forest organ clock, in Gothic styled oak case, 34½in. high.

20th century walnut cased mantel clock.

Clock case in green marble surmounted by a bronze figure, circa 1900, 39cm. high.

Viennese enamelled copper clock, 39cm. high, circa 1910.

Late 19th century clock, with ormolu mounts, 16in. high.

Late 19th century parcel gilt bronze lyre timepiece, with sunburst finial, 15½in. high.

46

Louis XVI ormolu and white marble mantel clock, 1ft.2in. high.

Mahogany cased clock with tulipwood banding, 25in. high.

Victorian barometer, clock and thermometer in oak case, 13in. high.

Preiss clock with marble base, 1930's, 37cm. high.

Late 19th century ormolu and bronze mantel clock with urn surmount.

Gilt bronze and porcelain mounted mantel clock, circa 1870, 16in. high.

French 19th century mantel clock.

Regency period mahogany cased mantel clock, 13in. high.

Viennese giltwood David and Goliath grande sonnerie mantel clock, 19in. high.

19th century white marble calendar mantel clock, 1ft. 4in. high.

Gilt and patinated bronze mantel clock, circa 1860, 18in. high, surmounted by a group of a Turk and his Horse.

Ithaca parlour model calendar clock in walnut case, with double dial.

French gilt and patinated bronze mantel clock, circa 1850-75, 1ft.10in. high.

Small Liberty & Co. pewter and enamel clock, 19.75cm. high, after 1903.

Ormolu Strutt timepiece with eight-day movement, signed 'Made by Thos. Cole', 5½in. high.

French Empire mantel clock in mahogany case, 50cm. high.

47

Brass cathedral skeleton clock signed C.Fiedemann, Liverpool.

Brass long duration timepiece skeleton clock, 12¾in. high.

Rare epicyclic skeleton clock, 10in. high, with a glass dome.

Brass skeleton clock, 13in. high.

Early skeleton clock by Hubert Sarton, 1ft. 5½in. high.

Unusual early 19th century skeleton clock of 'rafter' construction.

Large English striking skeleton clock, 22in. high.

Mid 19th century silvered brass skeleton timepiece, 12½in. high.

Rare chiming calendar skeleton clock, 1ft.7in. high.

Skeleton clock by Smith & Sons, Clerkenwell, 1ft. 4½in. high.

Good quality original Victorian skeleton timepiece, circa 1860.

English brass chiming skeleton clock, 20in. high.

Brass skeleton clock with enamel dial, circa 1890, 15¼in. high.

Unusual timepiece skeleton clock, 20in. high, with glass dome.

Unusual long duration Dutch skeleton clock, 2ft. 5in. high.

Astronomical skeleton clock, by James Gorham, 19th century.

48

Inlaid American eight day clock, circa 1890, 2ft. 4in. high.

Stained oak wall clock, Austrian, circa 1880, 38in. high.

Elaborate Victorian mahogany framed wall clock with brass pendulum.

Unusual mahogany wall timepiece by James McCabe, London, 8½in. high.

18th century French wall clock, 10½in. high.

Bristol example of an Act of Parliament clock by Wm. Preist.

Early striking clock by James Cowpe, London, circa 1665, 17in. high.

A 17th century Italian night clock in ebony case, 36½ x 22in.

Vienna regulator in dark walnut, 60in. high, circa 1900.

French giltwood cartel clock, signed J. Marti et Cie, 39in. high.

Early 20th century oak cased wall clock.

German Zappler clock, lacking pendulum, 11½in. high.

Dutch Friesland clock with painted dial, 27in. high.

Japanese weight driven wall timepiece, 16in. high.

Victorian papier mache wall clock by E. Fixary.

Mahogany wall regulator dial signed Dent, London, 4ft.4in. high.

49

Mid 18th century silver pair cased verge watch by Markwick of London, 73mm. diam.

Silver gilt and enamel duplex watch, 56mm. diam.

Silver quarter repeating alarm verge watch, signed Paul Beauvais, London, 55mm. diam.

Gold quarter repeating cylinder watch, by Ellicott of London, 1766, 49mm. diam.

Silver pair cased false pendulum verge watch by Marke Hawkins, 53mm. diam.

17th century verge watch by Joseph Chamberlain, Norwich, 52mm. diam.

Gold and enamel verge watch signed Breguet a Paris, 46mm. diam., circa 1790.

Swiss silver keyless mystery watch signed A. S. & P. Mysterieuse, Brevete S. G. D. G., 53mm. diam.

Swiss gold quarter repeating Jacquemart verge watch, 56mm. diam.

Oval silver watch for the Turkish Market, with Turkish numerals and subsidiary lunar dial, 63mm. long.

Silver pair cased verge watch, signed Thos. Gorsuch, Salop, 56mm. diam.

Silver pair cased verge watch by Markwick, London, circa 1710.

19th century gold quarter repeating independent centre seconds lever watch by Lepine, Paris, 47mm. diam.

Large silver pair cased verge watch, signed Wm. Smith, 81mm. diam.

Cartier gold breast pocket clip watch, 1930's, 5.3cm.

Pedometer watch signed by Spencer & Perkins, London, 52mm. diam., circa 1780.

19th century brass chamberstick with drip pan.

Cloisonne enamel quail, 5in. high, Qianlong period.

Set of three Victorian brass fire implements.

Late 18th century pierced brass footman with shaped front legs.

One of a pair of Liberty & Co. brass candlesticks, 13.5cm. high, circa 1900.

Victorian brass watering can.

A gallon copper measure.

20th century pressed brass magazine stand.

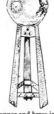

One of a pair of early 17th century brass candlesticks, 12in. high.

Two-handled cloisonne bowl, early 15th century, 8in. wide.

Copper and brass jardiniere on stand, Austrian, circa 1910, 53in. high.

Copper jar with a silver cover, surmounted by a lapis lazuli finial.

Late 19th century brass coal scuttle.

Late 19th century brass fire grate, 38in. wide.

Late 16th century Venetian brass charger, 19½in. diam.

W. Benson copper and brass kettle and burner, 11½in. high, 1890's.

51

DOLLS

A bisque headed character doll by Simon & Halbig.

Bisque headed doll with composition body and limbs stamped Thuringa, Germany.

German doll made by Herm. Steiner, 1912, 16in. long.

Armand Marseille bisque headed doll, 17in. high.

Jumeau bisque doll impressed Paris Fr.A.7, 15in. high.

A bisque headed child doll with jointed composition body, marked S.F.B.J. Paris 10, 23½in. tall.

French bisque Bru doll with paperweight eyes and kid body, 22in. tall.

Victorian doll impressed 'Fabrication Francaise al and Cie Limoges Cherie 5' 19in. high.

Bisque swivel headed doll with brown eyes, marked Heubach.

Simon & Halbig Japanese character doll.

American Ives & Co. clockwork walking doll, circa 1880, 9½in. high.

A George II painted wood doll, the face partly repainted and fingers damaged, 22in. high.

Parian doll with cloth body, 14in. tall.

Kammer & Reinhardt celluloid character doll.

Bisque headed Bebe doll by Bru, Paris, 24in. high.

Jumeau phonograph doll.

52

Early 18th century Anglo-Dutch walnut armoire, 65in. wide.

17th century Dutch oak armoire, 220cm. wide.

Mid 18th century Dutch walnut armoire, 67½in. wide.

Good late Louis XV provincial Bas'Armoire, circa 1765, 4ft.2in. wide.

Early 17th century North German fruitwood and oak armoire.

Mid 18th century Louis XV walnut provincial armoire, 4ft.9in. wide.

Late 16th century Flemish walnut armoire, 5ft.6in. wide.

19th century Dutch mahogany and marquetry wardrobe.

Dutch walnut and marquetry armoire with arched moulded cornice, 74in. wide.

Late 18th century North German or Scandinavian elm armoire, 84in. wide.

Late 17th century Italian walnut armoire with carved frieze, 46in. wide.

South German armoire.

18th century Spanish oak armoire with doors centred by roundels, 55½in. wide.

Mid 18th century French provincial oak armoire, 172cm. wide.

Late 18th century French provincial walnut armoire, 4ft.10in. wide.

18th century French armoire in oak veneered with tortoiseshell, 1.47m. wide.

Chippendale mahogany low-post bedstead, 52in. wide.

Mahogany and burl walnut double bed by Louis Majorelle, circa 1897, 68½in. wide.

Brass half-tester bed, circa 1900, 76in. wide.

Walnut half-tester bed, circa 1900, 83 x 58¼in.

Mid 20th century softwood and simulated bamboo tester bed, 72¾in. long.

One of a pair of Biedermeier beds in golden burr and straight cut elm, 6ft.5in. long, circa 1840.

Victorian mahogany bed with quilted headboard.

Part of a neo-Gothic suite of bedroom furniture.

George III four-poster bed.

Louis XVI carved walnut bed, 3ft.7½in. wide, circa 1790.

Victorian mahogany double bunk set.

Italian painted pinewood bed, 4ft.8in. wide, circa 1690.

Jacobean four-poster bed with hangings.

Unusual Regency mahogany folding campaign bed, 7ft. 4in. high.

18th century French bed, circa 1780, with shaped ends, canopy and bedspread, 8ft. 6in. high.

17th century tester bed with contemporary crewel work hangings.

A walnut square revolving bookcase, with pierced brass gallery, 3ft. high.

Early 19th century Regency mahogany revolving bookstand, 53in. high.

Late 19th century oak hanging bookcase with glazed doors, 3ft.8in. wide.

George III mahogany bookshelves supported on a central column with quadruple splayed feet.

A tortoiseshell bamboo bookcase with glazed doors.

Victorian pinewood bookshelves, 3ft. wide.

William IV pedestal bookcase in rosewood, 19½in. high.

19th century walnut open bookshelves with white marble top.

Ebonised and gilt bookcase, circa 1870.

George III breakfront mahogany library bookcase.

Late 18th century mahogany bookcase in the Chippendale style.

Breakfront mahogany bookcase with marquetry motifs on cornice, 9ft. high.

George IV library bookcase, circa 1825, 6ft.2in. wide.

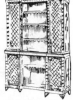

Regency mahogany bookcase by G. Oakley, 78½in. wide.

Oak bookcase with glazed upper half and carved doors.

19th century mahogany bookcase, 5ft.8in. wide.

Heavily carved Victorian oak bureau of four long graduated drawers with lion mask handles, 3ft. wide.

19th century Oriental carved teak bureau.

An Edwardian mahogany inlaid bureau with satinwood banded borders and four long drawers, on bracket feet, 2ft.6in. wide.

20th century oak bureau with oxidised handles.

Georgian mahogany bureau of good colour, 3ft. wide.

Rosewood and marquetry French bureau de dame, circa 1870, 65cm. wide.

An attractive bureau in golden ash crossbanded in walnut with a fine patina, 36in. wide, 41in. high, 20in. deep, circa 1740.

Louis XV provincial walnut bureau, circa 1750, 3ft.7in. wide.

Louis XV secretaire by Bernard II Van Risen Burgh, 26½in. wide.

English Queen Anne period oak bureau veneered with walnut, 94cm. wide.

North Italian walnut marquetry and parquetry bureau with fitted interior.

Early George III mahogany bureau on stand, 3ft. wide.

South German walnut bureau with inverted serpentine lower part, circa 1750, 3ft. 4in. wide.

Late 18th century Dutch mahogany cylinder bureau.

18th century Dutch marquetry double bureau, 4ft. 9in. wide.

Italian walnut marquetry bureau, circa 1780, 4ft.1in. wide.

20th century oak bureau bookcase with H stretcher.

18th century German walnut bureau cabinet.

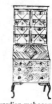

Edwardian mahogany bureau bookcase on cabriole legs.

George I red japanned bureau cabinet, 3ft.4in. wide.

George III mahogany cylinder bureau bookcase, circa 1780, 3ft.8in. wide.

Victorian bureau bookcase with glazed upper half.

Oak cylinder bureau cabinet, possibly German, circa 1780, 4ft.1in. wide.

Mid 18th century walnut and floral marquetry bureau cabinet.

Mid 18th century Sicilian bureau cabinet in walnut and marquetry, 1.07m. wide.

George III mahogany bureau bookcase, 3ft. 11in. wide.

A 19th century floral marquetry bureau bookcase on cabriole legs.

Georgian mahogany bureau cabinet.

Late 19th century satinwood bureau cabinet, 24½in. wide.

Dutch mahogany cylinder bureau bookcase.

Walnut bureau cabinet, circa 1715, with mirrors on the outside of the doors, 47½in. wide.

George I walnut bureau bookcase with broken circular pediment.

57

George III satinwood side cabinet, 3ft.2in. wide, circa 1770.

Mid 19th century mahogany side cabinet, 40in. wide, with hinged top.

Late 19th century carved oak coal cabinet with brass handles.

William and Mary seaweed marquetry cabinet on stand.

Edwardian rosewood music cabinet with a fall front and glazed door.

Art Nouveau style beechwood music cabinet.

17th century Austrian marquetry cabinet on stand, 31in. wide.

Charles II black and gold lacquer cabinet on stand, 50in. wide.

George III mahogany cabinet on stand with marquetry panels on the doors.

Fruitwood marquetry display cabinet, by Majorelle, circa 1910, 64cm. wide.

Small Art Nouveau breakfront cabinet, circa 1900, 58in. wide.

17th century German carved walnut cabinet, 64in. wide.

17th century Italian walnut cabinet, 63½in. wide.

Walnut dental cabinet, circa 1890, figured in burr-wood, 29¼in. wide.

Fine Oriental hardwood cabinet, gold panels with ivory carvings, 48in. wide.

Partly 17th century Dutch oak cabinet, 64in. wide.

Early 19th century mahogany music canterbury on short turned legs.

Early 19th century William IV rosewood canterbury, 20in. wide.

Burr-walnut music canterbury with nicely shaped partitions.

Reproduction mahogany, flat splat canterbury.

Victorian ebonised canterbury on short turned legs.

George III mahogany canterbury with flat splats.

Victorian mahogany canterbury in excellent condition.

Victorian rosewood canterbury with a drawer below.

Early 19th century Regency black-painted and gilded canterbury, 23in. wide.

Late George III mahogany plate canterbury, 1ft. 9in. long, circa 1805.

George III mahogany canterbury on slender turned tapered legs.

Regency rosewood canterbury with drawer, 48cm. wide.

Mid Victorian walnut stand with canterbury below, 2ft. 6in. wide.

Victorian burr-walnut music canterbury with fretted partitions and drawer in the base.

Victorian rosewood canterbury/whatnot.

Victorian bamboo canterbury with lacquered panels.

DINING CHAIRS

One of two rush-seated spindleback dining chairs.

One of a pair of Art Deco giltwood chairs, 94cm. high.

19th century child's chair in elm.

One of a set of six mahogany dining chairs, circa 1840.

One of a set of six chairs, by Thompson of Kilburn.

One of a set of six English rosewood drawingroom chairs, circa 1860.

One of a set of seven George III mahogany dining chairs.

19th century Continental carved teak chair on paw feet.

One of a pair of oak chairs, by Charles Rennie Mackintosh, circa 1900, 112cm. high.

One of a set of six painted and giltwood chairs, late 19th century, partly upholstered in petit point.

Late 18th century carved mahogany Chippendale style dining chair.

One of a set of six William IV dining chairs.

One of a set of seven Regency beechwood chairs, with an X-shaped splat.

One of a set of seven Dutch walnut marquetry chairs, mid 18th century.

One of a set of eight Regency ebonised and gilded dining chairs.

Queen Anne solid walnut single chair, circa 1710.

Victorian oak rocking chair.

One of a pair of armchairs, by Jacques Rhulmann, circa 1925.

Late Victorian oak easy chair with padded arms.

One of a pair of Victorian mahogany tub chairs on cabriole legs.

Large Art Deco giltwood tub chair, early 1920's.

Mahogany armchair, 1860's, on cabriole legs with castors.

Mid Victorian rosewood armchair.

Beechwood armchair, circa 1680, with padded back and seat.

George III mahogany chair, circa 1775.

Late Victorian easy chair.

Regency mahogany bereger, circa 1810.

A Victorian waxed rosewood spoon back easy chair on turned legs.

Fine George III mahogany saddle wing chair, 81cm. wide.

Fine Charles II giltwood armchair, on paw feet.

19th century highly carved hardwood easy chair.

George III mahogany library armchair of Chippendale style, arm supports carved with foliage,

61

ELBOW CHAIRS

Comb back Windsor arm-chair.

Victorian elm smoker's chair.

One of a set of eight George III mahogany dining chairs, circa 1780.

One of two carved and ebonised Oriental chairs.

George III mahogany armchair, circa 1785.

One of a set of eight early George III mahogany ladderback chairs, circa 1765.

One of a pair of George III giltwood open armchairs with rounded arched backs.

Queen Anne walnut armchair with solid vase-shaped splat and needlework seat.

One of a set of eleven George III mahogany dining chairs.

George III mahogany armchair, circa 1770.

One of a set of eight mid 18th century Dutch marquetry chairs.

One of a pair of heavily carved oak chairs.

One of a pair of George III mahogany armchairs, circa 1765.

Yew-wood high back Windsor elbow chair.

18th century mahogany lattice back armchair, with upholstered seat.

Charles II open armchair, 1662, with curved arms.

English oak chest of drawers, 39in. wide, circa 1930.

An Edwardian walnut chest of drawers with pierced brass handles.

Early 19th century Empire style chest with a figured marble top.

George III mahogany chest of three drawers, 92cm. wide.

Victorian figured mahogany bow-fronted chest on bun feet, 3ft.6in. wide.

Victorian Wellington chest veneered in rosewood.

19th century walnut military chest of drawers, 99cm. wide.

George II mahogany linen press and chest, 3ft.1in. wide, circa 1760.

Late 16th century Italian walnut chest, 3ft.8in. wide.

French Provincial walnut veneered chest of drawers, Charles X period, circa 1820.

Dutch marquetry and mahogany chest.

Jacobean oak chest with a pair of geometrically moulded doors, 3ft.3in. wide.

George II mahogany bachelor's chest, circa 1740, 3ft. wide.

Dutch marquetry chest of drawers, circa 1760, 3ft.1in. wide.

Small George III serpentine fronted mahogany chest, 3ft.3in. wide, circa 1785.

William and Mary marquetry chest of drawers.

Early Victorian mahogany chest on chest with boxwood string inlay and pressed brass handles.

George III mahogany tallboy on ogee feet with an arched pediment.

17th century oak chest in two sections, decorated all over, 38in. wide.

A fine quality 18th century walnut tallboy with fluted pilasters and a shaped apron.

George III mahogany bow-fronted tallboy, 104cm. wide.

Late 18th century oak chest on chest.

18th century Queen Anne burr-walnut cabinet on chest, 109cm. wide.

George I walnut tallboy, base with secretaire drawer, 42½in. wide.

Late 18th century flame mahogany chest on chest on ogee feet.

18th century walnut tallboy chest on bun feet.

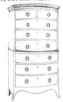

Late 18th century bow-fronted mahogany chest on chest on splayed feet.

Late 18th century mahogany chest on chest with a secretaire drawer.

19th century figured mahogany tallboy, 42in. high.

18th century mahogany chest on chest fitted with brushing slide.

George III oak tallboy, circa 1780, 3ft.10in. wide.

Late 18th century Irish mahogany tallboy on claw feet.

Chippendale walnut chest on stand, 42in. wide, circa 1760.

William and Mary chest on stand, 3ft.5in. wide, circa 1690.

Late 17th century Flemish ebonised and decorated chest on stand.

Early 18th century chest on stand in oyster walnut veneer inlaid with floral marquetry.

George I walnut chest on stand, 3ft.3in. wide, circa 1720.

William and Mary oyster veneered walnut cabinet on stand, 3ft.2in. wide, circa 1695.

Early 18th century walnut chest on stand.

A Queen Anne mulberry wood chest on stand with onion shaped feet.

Early 18th century walnut chest on stand.

Walnut chest on stand, circa 1710, 3ft.7in. wide.

George III oak chest on stand.

George I oak and walnut tall-boy on cabriole legs.

Portuguese rosewood chest on stand, 40¾in. wide.

Small oak chest on stand with moulded drawer fronts, 52in. high, circa 1780.

A fine William and Mary oyster veneered cabinet on stand with barley twist legs and cross stretchers.

American fruitwood high-boy on cabriole legs.

CHIFFONIERS

Early 19th century figured mahogany chiffonier with panelled doors.

Fine quality rosewood chiffonier, 45in. wide.

Late 19th century oak cupboard.

Victorian mahogany chiffonier with arched panel doors.

William IV rosewood side cabinet, 5ft.6in. wide, circa 1835.

Edwardian walnut chiffonier with carved cupboard doors.

Early 19th century rosewood chiffonier with unusual fretted door panels, 15½in. deep, 54in. wide, 49in. tall.

Late 19th century mahogany chiffonier.

Victorian mahogany chiffonier, 3ft.1in. wide, with shelves above.

One of a pair of 19th century satinwood chiffoniers with Wedgwood jasper plaques.

Regency marquetry and brass inlaid chiffonier.

Solid satinwood chiffonier, circa 1830, 45in. long.

Regency rosewood and parcel gilt chiffonier with two shelves, 43in. wide.

Regency rosewood chiffonier with inlaid cut brass, 43in. wide.

Regency rosewood chiffonier with concave outline.

One of a pair of Regency brass inlaid rosewood chiffoniers, by Louis Gaigneur.

18th century German oak marriage trunk, 56in. long, dated 1767.

A highly carved 19th century camphor wood chest.

Old elm chest, possibly 14th century.

17th century carved oak coffer, 120cm. wide.

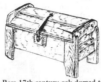

Rare 17th century oak domed top ark of plank construction, 97cm. wide.

George II walnut and mahogany chest with hinged lid, circa 1740, 3ft.9in. wide.

17th century oak and yew small coffer on gothic arcaded trestle supports, 30in. wide.

George II black japanned chest, mid 18th century, with later stand, 4ft. 1½in. wide.

Dutch colonial nadun wood chest, 40in. wide

18th century Indian Indo-Portuguese blanket chest, heavily carved, 58in. long.

17th century Spanish iron chest, 31in. wide, with floral painted panels.

Late 19th century walnut coffer.

Late 18th century dark green leather hide covered coaching trunk, 36in. long.

Late 15th century Piedmontese walnut cassone, 4ft.8in. wide.

Late 18th century pine coffer on bracket feet.

COMMODE CHESTS

18th century Danish walnut and parcel gilt bombe commode, 78cm. wide.

Louis XV commode in marquetry decorated with fire gilt bronze, after Duplessis Pere.

A Louis XV kingwood parquetry commode of serpentine shape with ormolu mounts.

Black lacquer and parcel gilt commode, 44in. wide.

Late 18th century Italian rosewood and marquetry commode.

18th century Dutch walnut and floral marquetry commode with shaped top.

Marquetry commode with serpentine top, 46¼in. wide.

Louis XIV marquetry and ormolu mounted commode, 122cm. wide.

Empire mahogany commode with black marble top, 51½in. wide.

Edwardian satinwood commode with convex centre section.

North Italian serpentine commode, late 18th century.

Louis XV/XVI transitional ormolu mounted marquetry commode, stamped C. Wolff.

Spanish mahogany commode with white marble top, circa 1825, 4ft.1in. wide.

One of a pair of Biedermeier bird's eye maple commodes, 41in. wide.

Danish walnut and giltwood commode in two parts, 4ft. 2in. wide, circa 1750.

George III satinwood and marquetry commode, 53¼in. wide.

68

Early 19th century mahogany night commode, 25½in. wide.

19th century French walnut pot cupboard on shaped legs.

French directoire bidet with marble top, 52cm. wide.

Victorian mahogany one step commode on short turned legs.

Victorian bamboo and cane pot cupboard.

Victorian mahogany commode complete with liner.

Edwardian inlaid mahogany bedside cupboard.

George IV mahogany bedside commode with fall front, 67cm.

19th century mahogany inlaid commode with cupboard and drawers, 1ft.11in. wide.

Late 18th century satinwood bedside table on square tapering legs.

Late 18th century mahogany, tambour fronted, night commode, with carrier handles.

A fine early 19th century travelling commode with sunken brass carrying handles and a Spode basin.

18th century marquetry bedside cupboard, 2ft.6in. high.

19th century mahogany lift-up commode with ebony inlay.

Victorian mahogany pot cupboard with fluted sides.

Late 18th century Chippendale style mahogany night table, 23in. wide, with tray top.

CORNER CUPBOARDS

Late 18th century pine corner cupboard of good colour.

George III walnut veneered corner cupboard with swan neck pediment.

19th century carved oak corner cupboard.

George I black lacquer hanging corner cabinet, 36½in. high.

Late 18th century mahogany hanging corner cupboard.

One of a pair of late 18th century mahogany cabinets with shaped marble tops.

A mahogany wall corner cupboard, with swan neck pediment and dentil cornice above trellis glazed door, 2ft.6in. wide.

One of a pair of mid 18th century Louis XV ormolu mounted kingwood parquetry encoignures, 3ft.0½in. high.

Carved and painted corner cupboard with pierced cornice, circa 1760, 2ft. 5in. wide.

George III stripped pine corner cupboard with shaped shelves.

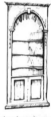

Georgian domed corner cupboard, circa 1740.

George I mahogany corner cupboard, 4ft. wide.

Edwardian mahogany corner cabinet, 40in. wide.

Late 18th century inlaid mahogany corner cupboard.

Georgian mahogany corner display cabinet, 3ft.6in. wide.

18th century Dutch marquetry corner cupboard.

Mid 17th century oak court cupboard with carved frieze, 4ft.6in. wide.

Mid 19th century oak court cupboard, 51in. wide.

Stained oak court cupboard, made in the mid 19th century.

Commonwealth oak court cupboard with moulded cornice, 67in. wide.

17th century oak court cupboard, 61in. wide.

Late 17th century Welsh oak duodarn, 48in. wide.

Commonwealth oak court cupboard with moulded rectangular top, 44½in. wide, inlaid with bone and mother-of-pearl.

Late 17th century Welsh oak court cupboard.

Queen Anne oak court cupboard, circa 1710, 4ft.3in. wide.

Bleached oak court cupboard, 57in. wide, circa 1860.

Charles I oak court cupboard, circa 1630, 3ft. 8½in. wide.

Continental oak court cupboard, heavily carved and of good size.

17th century French oak dressoire with geometric inlay and blind fret decoration, 52in. wide.

18th century oak court cupboard with fielded panels.

20th century Jacobean style oak court cupboard.

Continental court cupboard with fitted drawer and under tray.

CRADLES

Victorian wickerwork cradle.

A Normandy carved oak cradle with openwork end bobbin panels, 3ft.4in. wide.

Dutch child's cradle in the form of a sledge, 22in. long.

19th century Breton style cradle, with turned finials, 90cm. wide.

Late 18th century mahogany crib.

Oak cradle with carved lunettes and lozenge decoration.

A 19th century painted wood boat cradle.

George IV mahogany cradle, 3ft.1in. wide, circa 1825.

Victorian cast iron cradle on castors.

19th century mahogany crib with carved end, 97cm. long.

17th century Continental oak crib.

A 19th century Indian cradle.

Early 19th century pinewood cradle on rockers, 36in. long.

Regency caned mahogany cradle, 3ft.11in. high, circa 1820.

17th century oak cradle with pointed hood, 3ft. long.

Mid 19th century painted cradle, 38½in. long.

Kidney-shaped Empire style child's cradle, circa 1800, 39in. long.

Early 17th century hooded oak baby's cradle.

A Victorian brass crib.

Early 19th century parcel gilt mahogany cradle, 3ft.11in. wide.

A fine Victorian walnut credenza, with shaped ends and ormolu mounts

Walnut side cabinet, circa 1870, 4ft.9in. wide.

Victorian walnut credenza with concave ends and a glazed centre door.

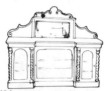

Marquetry kingwood porcelain mounted side cabinet, circa 1870, 82in. wide.

Italian Renaissance walnut credenza, circa 1580, 4ft. 9½in. wide.

19th century rosewood breakfront credenza.

19th century French red Buhl breakfront cabinet, 6ft. 9in. wide.

Italian walnut credenza on plinth base, 45in. wide.

Ebonised porcelain and gilt bronze mounted display cabinet, 1860's, 72in. wide.

Good walnut side cabinet, 1880's, 76in. wide.

Mid 19th century walnut side cabinet, 67in. wide.

Victorian burr-walnut breakfront credenza with canted corners, 5ft.7in. wide.

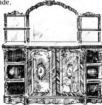

French ebonised and inlaid breakfront three door dwarf cabinet decorated with Sevres type oval figure scene, porcelain plaques and ormolu mounts, 60 ins. long

Mid 19th century walnut credenza with marquetry designs.

Good burr-walnut side cabinet, 1860's, 72in. wide.

Charles I oak food cupboard.

18th century Continental carved walnut bread cupboard with spindled front.

Late Victorian carved oak buffet.

Regency walnut cupboard with moulded top, circa 1730, 4ft.7in. wide.

Mid 17th century oak cupboard, 4ft.1in. wide.

'Mouseman' oak cupboard, 36in. wide, circa 1936-40.

Late 19th century oak side table with cupboard.

18th century Normandy Regency bridal cupboard in oak.

George III mahogany clothes press, 51in. wide.

Mid 19th century carved oak cupboard, 145cm. wide.

18th century Dutch mahogany linen press, 66in. wide.

German walnut parquetry cupboard, circa 1740, 6ft. 2in. wide.

Fine Art Nouveau mahogany sideboard cupboard, French, circa 1900, 59in. wide.

Mid 18th century Dutch marquetry cupboard, 5ft.8in. wide.

17th century Flemish oak cupboard, 68¾in. wide.

18th century oak settle with panelled cupboard doors.

Mid 19th century walnut Davenport, 32 x 23½in.

Walnut harlequin Davenport, 1860's, 23in. wide.

Victorian rosewood Davenport, 53cm. wide.

Mid 19th century walnut Davenport, 21¼in. wide.

Late 19th century walnut Davenport, 24in. wide.

Attractive George III mahogany Davenport.

Unusual walnut Davenport writing table, circa 1870, 20¾in. wide.

Walnut harlequin Davenport, circa 1860, 23in. wide.

Burr-walnut inlaid ebonised Davenport, 22in. wide, circa 1860-80.

Victorian burr-walnut piano top Davenport desk.

Walnut Davenport, circa 1860, 37½in. wide, with central turned balustrade.

Walnut and burr-walnut Davenport, 1870's.

Satinwood crossbanded mahogany Davenport, 1ft. 9in. wide, 1900's.

William IV rosewood Davenport, circa 1830, 1ft.9in. wide.

Oak Davenport with three quarter gallery, 1880's, 24in. wide.

Regency rosewood Davenport surmounted by a brass gallery, 17in. wide.

DISPLAY CABINETS

19th century burr-walnut display cabinet with brass escutcheons.

19th century heart-shaped specimen table, inlaid with marquetry.

19th century mahogany specimen table on cabriole legs with ormolu mounts.

Mahogany vitrine 34 x 17in., 1880-1900.

Early display cabinet, by Charles Rennie Mackintosh, circa 1895.

An Edwardian mahogany display cabinet, with mirror backed central and lower scroll backed glazed side cupboards.

Chippendale mahogany display cabinet with a blind fret cornice, 57in. wide, circa 1890.

Early George III mahogany display cabinet, 4ft. wide.

19th century Chinese hardwood display cabinet.

French 'Vernis Martin' vitrine decorated by Paeli.

Fine quality 19th century carved mahogany display cabinet.

Mahogany vitrine, circa 1895, 68in. high.

Louis XV silver display cabinet with gilt bronze mounts.

Finely carved late 18th century Oriental hardwood display cabinet.

Walnut and parcel gilt cabinet on stand with glazed top, 40in. wide.

Early 18th century Dutch mahogany and marquetry display cabinet, 5ft.6in. wide.

76

George III oak dresser, circa 1780, 6ft.4in. wide.

Georgian oak low dresser with moulded rectangular top crossbanded in mahogany, 73½in. wide.

George III oak dresser with plate racks, 5ft.7in. wide.

Flemish 17th century oak dresser fitted with three drawers, 7ft. long.

Early 18th century country made oak dresser, 72in. wide.

Late Georgian Welsh oak dresser, 72in. wide.

Early 20th century oak dresser with brass handles.

Late 17th century oak dresser with open shelves.

Anglesey dresser in oak banded with mahogany.

Victorian carved oak dresser with pot cupboard.

Mid 18th century oak dresser base, 5ft.6in. wide.

18th century French provincial oak dresser.

18th century oak clock dresser, dial signed Nathaniel Olding, Wincanton, 96in. wide.

Victorian 'Dog Kennel' dresser, circa 1850, 63in. wide.

18th century Lancashire oak and pine dresser.

Louis XV decorated cartonnier in fruitwood.

DUMB WAITERS

A small Edwardian mahogany serving table on a tripod base.

19th century two-tier dumb waiter with marquetry and ormolu mounts.

William IV period mahogany dumb waiter of three shelves, 42in. high.

George III three-tier mahogany dumb waiter on a tripod base with ball and claw feet.

HALL STANDS

Late 19th century oak hall stand with brass fittings.

Victorian mahogany hat and coat stand.

Edwardian oak hall stand.

Victorian carved oak hallstand, 7ft. high.

JARDINIERES

Mid 18th century mahogany jardiniere, 28¾in. high.

Rosewood marquetry jardiniere, circa 1900, possibly French.

19th century black lacquer and gilt jardiniere. $280

Mid 19th century japanned jardiniere, 2ft. 1in. wide.

LOWBOYS

Early Victorian walnut lowboy with claw and ball cabriole legs, 30in. wide.

An 18th century mahogany lowboy, 29in. wide.

Late 18th century mahogany lowboy on square cut cabriole legs.

18th century Dutch marquetry lowboy, 84cm. wide.

78

One-piece mahogany pedestal writing desk, circa 1760, 81cm. wide.

Small oak kneehole desk of nine drawers, 45in. wide.

George II mahogany kneehole desk with serpentine top, 44½in. wide.

Early 20th century oak tambour top desk.

George II mahogany kneehole desk with leather lined top, 49½in. wide.

George II mahogany kneehole desk, 3ft.2in. wide, circa 1760.

19th century oak pedestal desk with tooled leather top.

Victorian mahogany cylinder top pedestal writing desk.

George IV mahogany kneehole desk, top inset with leather, 3ft.5½in. wide.

Continental kneehole desk in parquetry applied walnut, circa 1680, with hinged top, 43in. wide.

Late 19th century mahogany desk with tooled leather top.

An unusual 18th century walnut kneehole desk on bracket feet.

George II padoukwood kneehole writing table with leather writing surface, 2ft.11½in. wide.

Late 18th century Sheraton inlaid and decorated satinwood kneehole desk.

Late 18th century inlaid mahogany cylinder desk, 44in. wide.

William and Mary period walnut kneehole desk with ebony arabesque marquetry inlay.

79

SCREENS

American leaded glass firescreen, circa 1900, 45¼in. high.

Early 20th century ebonised and giltwood three-fold screen.

Early 20th century oak firescreen.

Three-fold painted screen, circa 1910, panel signed Jules Vernon-Fair.

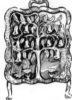

John Pearson bronze and wrought iron fire-screen, circa 1906, 27½in. high.

Late 18th century giltwood firescreen with needlework panel.

Early 19th century six-leaf screen, 70½in. high.

Mahogany pole screen on tripod supports with tapestry in rococo frame.

Giltwood and stained glass screen, circa 1900, 62in. wide.

Mahogany and leather five-fold screen, circa 1900, 85in. wide overall.

Late 19th century brass and glass firescreen.

Jennens and Bettridge papier mache firescreen, 41in. high, circa 1850.

Japanese ivory table screen, 12½in. high.

Louis XVI giltwood screen with eight panels.

Lacquer panelled two-fold screen with carved ivory ornamentation.

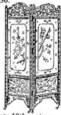

Late 19th century hardwood four-fold screen, 73in. high.

80

Mahogany secretaire of the Sheraton period, interior with concave drawers and inlay, 43in. high, circa 1800.

American 'Wells Fargo' desk by Wootton & Co., 42½in. wide.

Hepplewhite mahogany secretaire inlaid with rosewood and satinwood.

Victorian rosewood secretaire Wellington chest.

Italian walnut secretaire a abattant, 2ft.9in. wide, circa 1790.

South German mahogany secretaire, 1840's, 39in. wide.

Oak secretaire, by M. H. Baillie-Scott with pewter and marquetry inlay, 46in. high.

Early 19th century Dutch mahogany secretaire.

Walnut veneered fall front cabinet of William and Mary design, 40in. wide.

Writing cabinet of dark stained wood, by Charles Rennie Mackintosh, 37¼in. wide.

Empire ormolu mounted mahogany secretaire a abattant, circa 1810, 3ft.2¼in. wide.

French secretaire a abattant in oak veneered with tulipwood and kingwood, 58cm. wide, by Jean-Francois Dubot.

16th century Spanish walnut vargueno, 4ft.2in. wide, later stand.

18th century oak fall front escritoire on chest.

Good Liege secretaire cabinet in burr-elm with ebonised and walnut banding, circa 1730, 3ft.11in. wide.

George III mahogany secretaire chest, 42in. wide.

SECRETAIRE BOOKCASES

Ebonised secretaire bookcase, circa 1880, 42¾in. wide.

Late 19th century carved mahogany secretaire bookcase with astragal glazed doors.

Empire secretaire bookcase with fold down flap.

Satinwood secretaire with scalloped gallery, circa 1900, 27½in. wide.

Unusual American mahogany secretaire, 40in. wide, circa 1860-80.

Chippendale period mahogany secretaire bookcase with ogee feet.

Late 17th century green lacquered double domed secretaire cabinet, 1.04m. wide.

Georgian secretaire cabinet, 4ft.6in. wide.

Early 18th century walnut secretaire cabinet.

Early Victorian figured mahogany breakfront secretaire bookcase, 230cm. wide.

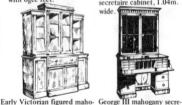

George III mahogany secretaire bookcase, 7ft.7½in. high, 4ft.1in. wide.

George III mahogany breakfront secretaire bookcase.

George III mahogany secretaire open bookcase, 81cm. wide.

Early 19th century secretaire bookcase with carved pilasters and vase shaped feet.

Queen Anne walnut secretaire cabinet, 2ft.5in. wide, circa 1710, on later bun feet.

English secretaire cabinet, circa 1780, veneered with sycamore, rosewood and fruitwood, 1.2m. wide.

An early Victorian walnut framed settee.

Victorian rosewood framed chaise longue on turned legs.

Edwardian inlaid mahogany settee on cabriole legs.

Victorian mahogany settee on cabriole legs, 4ft. 6in. wide.

Ash settle, designed for Liberty & Co., circa 1900, 51in. wide.

Chippendale mahogany chair-back settee, circa 1880-1900, 72in. wide.

Victorian mahogany scroll end settee on turned legs.

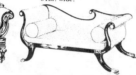

A nicely proportioned Regency mahogany framed couch with brass inlay, splay feet and claw castors.

Victorian, rosewood, barley twist framed, couch with button backrest and turned feet with brass castors.

Louis XVI gilt canape with petal-moulded frame, 4ft.5in. wide.

Oak and beaten copper inlaid settle, 1900-1910.

Louis XV beechwood canape on moulded cabriole legs, 5ft.1in. wide.

Charles II walnut day bed, circa 1660, 5ft. long with caned back.

A carved oak hall settle, 56in. long.

Russian amboyna wood chaise longue with gilt enrichments.

83

SHELVES

One of a pair of late 19th century mahogany hanging shelves, 36¼in. wide,

19th century mahogany hanging book-shelves with ornate 'S' scroll supports.

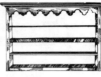

Late 18th century oak two-shelved hanging plate rack.

One of a pair of mahogany corner shelves, mid 19th century, 34in. high.

Victorian stripped pine glazed hanging cabinet, 2ft.6in. wide.

Chippendale style mahogany wallshelves with fretted sides, circa 1760.

One of a pair of late George III giltwood eagle wall brackets, circa 1800, 1ft.3in. high.

Mahogany Regency set of hanging shelves with carved cresting, circa 1820, 26½in. wide.

STEPS

Late 18th century mahogany library steps on short turned legs.

George III mahogany library steps with brass fittings.

Set of George III folding library steps, 7ft.5½in. high, open.

George III antique oak steps, circa 1790, 17¼in. wide, original bracket feet.

Mahogany eight tread library steps with handrails, converting to a rectangular top table, on chamfered legs, 40in.

A set of early Victorian mahogany library steps which convert to a small arm elbow chair.

A set of fine Regency mahogany bed steps, 26in. high, 28in. deep, 19in. wide.

George III oak and satinwood library steps, 7ft.8in. high.

84

Large sideboard in pale walnut, 1930's, 175cm. wide.

An Edwardian bow-fronted sideboard, on cabriole legs, with a gadrooned edge.

18th century mahogany chest sideboard inlaid in the Sheraton manner.

Victorian mahogany sideboard with cellarette drawer.

George III mahogany sideboard, with reeded projecting corners and original brass knobs.

19th century painted satinwood sideboard.

George III bow-fronted sideboard.

Mid 19th century oak sideboard, heavily carved, 90in. wide.

Small 20th century Jacobean style oak sideboard.

George III satinwood breakfronted serving table, 71in. wide.

Mid 19th century rosewood sideboard, 68 x 66in.

Late 18th century padoukwood pedestal sideboard.

Early Victorian mahogany pedestal sideboard with a shaped backboard.

George III mahogany bow-front sideboard.

Attractively figured Sheraton serpentine fronted sideboard.

85

Charles II walnut stool, 3ft. 3in. wide, circa 1680.

A superb Regency stool with carved gilt rope feet.

Small Regency rosewood footstool.

Edwardian mahogany stool on tapered legs with spade feet.

James I oak joint stool, circa 1610, 1ft.6in. wide.

Victorian rosewood revolving top piano stool.

Sheraton style mahogany box strung and upholstered lyre shaped window seat.

George I walnut stool with drop-in seat, 1ft.9in. wide, circa 1720.

Second Empire mahogany stool with drop-in seat, 19½in. square, circa 1870.

A mahogany inlaid oblong piano stool on square tapered legs.

Small Victorian upholstered footstool on bun feet.

20th century beech framed piano stool.

Oak stool as used by a lacemaker with under satchet for tools.

Victorian wind-up piano stool, upholstered in dralon.

One of a pair of folding stools by Jean-Baptiste Sene, circa 1786.

An Edwardian, rush seated, oblong footstool.

Late 19th century ebonised stool on turned legs.

A Queen Anne oak close stool with simulated drawers.

A superb mid 19th century brass X frame stool, 2ft. 5in. wide.

Unusual stained walnut stool, circa 1890, 43in. high.

Part of an Edwardian inlaid seven-piece mahogany suite.

Part of a late 19th century walnut nine-piece suite with upholstered seats and backs.

Victorian carved walnut parlour set of seven pieces.

Part of an Art Deco drawingroom suite, late 1930's, upholstered in velvet.

Part of a French giltwood chateau suite of Louis XV design, comprising a canape, four fauteuils, banquette stool, firescreen and three-fold screen.

Victorian rosewood inlaid envelope card table with drawer and undershelf.

Regency mahogany card table.

Early Victorian serpentine front burr-walnut folding top card table.

Compact rosewood card table, circa 1860.

19th century mahogany fold-over top card table.

Late George II mahogany card table, circa 1755, 2ft. 11½in. wide.

Burr-walnut card table, 1860's, 35in. wide.

Late 17th century walnut games table with fold-over top, 33in. long.

19th century marquetry and kingwood swivel top card table.

George IV satinwood card table, circa 1825, 3ft. wide.

Rosewood card table, 1840's, 36in. wide.

Georgian mahogany card table, on cabriole legs, 2ft.4in. wide.

George II red walnut tea or games table, circa 1740, 2ft.8in. wide.

George II semi-circular mahogany card table, 1ft. 8in. wide, circa 1740.

Hepplewhite mahogany card table, 3ft. wide, on French cabriole legs.

Victorian burr-walnut folding top card table on cabriole legs.

Italian painted consol table on hoof feet, circa 1790.

Victorian cast iron consol table with marble top.

One of a pair of 18th century gilt consol tables attributed to T. Johnson.

Mid 18th century Genoese painted consol table, 4ft. 1in. wide.

Early 18th century George I giltwood consol table, 48in. wide.

Mid 18th century German white painted and parcel gilt consol table, 27½in. wide.

Early 18th century German carved oak consol table.

A small mid 18th century giltwood consol table with a figured marble top, 25in. wide.

Louis XV giltwood consol table with brown and white marble top, 40½in. wide.

George II giltwood consol table with an eagle support and figured marble top.

Giltwood consol table with marble top, probably Scandinavian, circa 1770, 2ft.8in. wide.

Giltwood consol table, circa 1765, by Robt. Adam.

Charles X mahogany consol table, circa 1825, 4ft.4in. wide.

One of a pair of Empire ormolu mounted bronze and mahogany consols, 1ft.6in. wide.

William IV consol table in rosewood, 3ft.2in. wide.

Wood and perspex consol table, 1930's, 91.25cm. high.

English walnut dining table, 60½in. diam., circa 1935.

Early Victorian marquetry centre table, 64in. diam., circa 1840.

19th century oak dining table with carved frieze.

George III mahogany rent table, 42in. diam.

Regency mahogany centre table, circa 1815, 4ft.1in. diam.

18th century satinwood table inlaid with bog wood.

Walnut breakfast table, circa 1860, 53½in. wide.

Mahogany octagonal breakfast table, circa 1880, with inlaid top.

19th century mahogany snap-top table on tripod base.

Regency rosewood tilt-top table inlaid with brass.

French marquetry occasional table with gilt bronze scroll feet, mid 19th century, 81.5cm. high.

Burr-walnut circular breakfast table, 1860's, 48in. diameter.

20th century oak draw-leaf table on twist supports.

Early Victorian figured mahogany breakfast table, 121cm. diam.

18th century mahogany breakfast table on reeded legs, 4ft.6in. x 3ft.4in.

Ebonised centre table, circa 1870, 51in. wide.

Small late 18th century bow-fronted mahogany dressing table.

George III mahogany dressing table with real and dummy drawers below.

Part of a suite of Betty Joell satinwood bedroom furniture, circa 1930.

Liberty & Co. oak toilet table, 38½in. wide, circa 1900.

Georgian mahogany dressing and writing table, 36in. wide, 23in. deep, 31in. high.

Queen Anne black and gold lacquer union suite with bureau base, 21½in. wide.

Fitted satinwood kneehole dressing table, 35in. wide.

Dressing table, by Emile Jacques Rhulmann, circa 1920, 43½in. wide.

Victorian chest of drawers with fitted top drawer, marble top and toilet mirror.

Georgian red walnut dressing table with rising top, 2ft.7in. wide.

Sheraton period mahogany 'D' table, 36in. wide, circa 1780.

A fine quality Victorian mahogany dressing table.

Louis XV kingwood and tulipwood parquetry coiffeuse, 3ft. 1in. wide, circa 1760.

High Kitsch dressing table, 161cm. high, 1930's.

A kidney-shaped dressing table.

Bamboo and rattan dressing table, circa 1880-1900, 37in. wide.

Regency mahogany extending dining table, circa 1815, 8ft.4in. long.

17th century Italian walnut centre table.

George II mahogany drop-leaf table, 3ft. high, circa 1750.

Queen Anne mahogany drop-leaf dining table, 48in. wide.

Dutch mahogany and marquetry drop-leaf table, circa 1760, 4ft. wide.

Rare yew-wood envelope table with flap supported by a loper, circa 1730.

George III rectangular mahogany and cross-banded drop-leaf spider gateleg table.

George II period red walnut drop-leaf table, 30in. wide.

19th century Cuban mahogany drop-leaf table.

A Victorian ebonised drop-leaf table, the oval top with boxwood stringing and stylised paterae, 4ft.3in. wide.

Italian walnut drop-leaf table, circa 1610, 3ft.11½in. long.

17th century oak well table on turned legs.

George III mahogany dining table, circa 1810.

George II mahogany oval gateleg table, 104cm. wide.

Country made oak drop-leaf table, circa 1820.

Late 18th century mahogany drop-leaf dining table with six legs.

92

Mid 17th century carved oak gateleg table, 72in. wide, open.

An 18th century oak gateleg table, with turned legs.

Charles I oak gateleg table, circa 1640, 5ft.6in. extended.

A small Charles II oak gateleg table, 1ft.9in. wide.

Charles II oak gateleg table, circa 1670, 3ft.2in. wide.

Charles II large oak gateleg table, circa 1680, 5ft.10in., open.

William and Mary oak gateleg table, circa 1690, 4ft. 6in. open.

Mid 17th century oak credence table with carved frieze.

Louis XIV walnut double gateleg table, circa 1680, 4ft. 11in. open.

Rare 17th century oak gateleg table with plain gate supports, 27½in. high.

Late 17th century oak oval gateleg dining table, 4ft.8½in. opened.

Charles II oak gateleg table, 3ft.1in. wide, circa 1680.

17th century oak gateleg table, circa 1670, 26½in. diam.

A Victorian oval gateleg table, with two leaves, on turned legs, full width 3ft. 2in.

A large 18th century gateleg table with drawer, 5ft.2in. wide.

Victorian carved oak gateleg table on barley twist supports.

George III mahogany three pedestal dining table, 51 x 152in. extended.

Oak dining table by J.J. Joass, 66in. long, circa 1940.

Early 18th century Continental walnut dining table on shaped legs, 6ft. long.

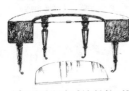

A fine, semi-circular, Irish drinking table, with additional flap.

18th century D-ended mahogany dining table.

Mid-19th century American pitch pine refectory table, 96½in. long.

George III mahogany hunting table, 8ft. 10in. long, circa 1780.

19th century mahogany extending dining table on claw and ball feet.

Solid mahogany dining table which makes two breakfast tables, circa 1830.

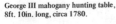

George III D-end mahogany dining table, 9ft. 9in. long extended.

Fine mahogany dining table with lattice underframing, George IV, circa 1825, 7ft. 6in. x 4ft. 5in.

17th century oak and beechwood centre table, 83in. long.

Early 17th century oak drawleaf dining table, 133in. wide.

Late George III figured mahogany twin pedestal dining table, turned columns and splayed supports.

Single plank oak trestle-end dining table, 8ft.2in. long, with single stretcher.

Rosewood and marquetry occasional table, late 19th century, 18¼in. wide.

Late George II mahogany tripod table, 2ft. high.

Small George II marble topped red walnut table, 1ft. 10in. wide.

Rosewood coffee table by Jacques Rhulmann, circa 1925, 26½in. diam.

George III mahogany circular supper table, 29½in. diam.

George III mahogany architect's table, circa 1765, 2ft. 11½in. wide.

Circular Victorian table in prime condition.

A circular garden table on three cast iron legs, 2ft. diam.

George III mahogany drum top table, 3ft.7in. diam.

Solid walnut centre table, circa 1740, 2ft.9in. wide, possibly Portuguese.

19th century Burmese carved teak wood circular table with pierced apron, 68cm. diam.

Chippendale period mahogany architect's table.

Marquetry centre table, stretchers edged with bone and ebony, 45in. wide.

Late 18th century walnut cricket table.

Set of four marquetry tables with glass tops, circa 1900, by Galle.

Early 1920's marble topped Art Deco occasional table, 54.5cm. square.

95

PEMBROKE TABLES

George III satinwood 'Harlequin' Pembroke table, 36¼in. wide, open.

George III mahogany 'butterfly' shaped Pembroke table, 37½in. wide, open.

Late Victorian stripped pine Pembroke table with drawer, on turned legs.

George III faded mahogany and crossbanded rectangular Pembroke table, 77cm. wide.

George III satinwood Pembroke table, circa 1780, 2ft. 10in. wide.

George III mahogany supper table, with wire grills to the lower section, 39¾in. wide.

19th century satinwood Pembroke table, 32½in. wide.

George III mahogany 'butterfly' shaped Pembroke table, 2ft.6in. wide, circa 1780.

SIDE TABLES

Empire simulated rosewood side table, 49in. wide.

James I oak side table with bulbous supports, circa 1610.

19th century boulle side table with ormolu mounts.

Stained oak side table, circa 1880, 38in. wide.

Late 17th century oak side table, 33in. wide.

18th century giltwood side table on square tapered legs.

Fine oak side table, circa 1830, 31in. wide.

George II walnut side table, 2ft.6in. wide, circa 1730.

Regency brass inlaid sofa table in rosewood.

Regency mahogany sofa table, 5ft. wide open, circa 1810.

Edwardian mahogany sofa table, 58in. wide.

Mahogany and marquetry sofa table, circa 1890, 44in. wide.

William IV rosewood sofa table, 88cm. wide.

Regency mahogany sofa table, circa 1815, 5ft.10in. wide.

Regency brass inlaid rosewood sofa table, circa 1815, 3ft.7in. wide.

Regency rosewood sofa table/games table with satinwood crossbanded top.

SUTHERLAND TABLES

Victorian burr-walnut Sutherland table with shaped feet.

Sutherland table in mahogany with brass inlay.

A mahogany Sutherland tea table with two folding leaves, on turned supports, 3ft. wide.

Burr-walnut Sutherland table, circa 1860, 41½in. wide.

A rosewood inlaid oblong two-tier table with folding leaves and satinwood banded borders, 2ft. wide.

Solid mahogany Sutherland table on turned legs, circa 1840.

Walnut Sutherland table, 22¼in., circa 1880.

Mahogany inlaid and satinwood banded Sutherland tea table on turned legs, 2ft. wide.

97

Victorian chinoiserie lacquer work table, 28in. high.

20th century Carine parquetry games table, 37in. wide.

Rosewood work table, circa 1850, 30 x 22½in.

Victorian rosewood work table.

Victorian rosewood work table with sliding bag.

Russian ebony and boulle games table, late 18th century, 30½in. wide.

William IV brass inlaid rosewood chess table, 1ft. 9in. wide, circa 1830.

English walnut combined work and games table with divided swivelling top, 1850's, 28in. high.

Victorian fitted burr-walnut work table.

Sheraton period tulipwood tricoteuse of French influence, 27 x 16in.

Late 18th century mahogany games and writing table, 75 x 109 x 56cm.

Victorian rosewood needlework table.

19th century work table with marquetry decoration, on fine turned legs.

Good quality early Victorian burr-walnut work table with a chess board top.

17th century South German games table complete with games.

George III satinwood work table, 1ft.8in. wide, circa 1790.

98

Antique mahogany architect's table with ratchet writing surface.

Art Deco galuchat and ivory, lady's writing table, circa 1930.

Late 19th century ormolu mounted kingwood bureau plat, 53in. wide.

Late 19th century oak folding desk.

Victorian pine and cast iron school desk and chair.

Edwardian inlaid rosewood writing table with inset leather top, 2ft.6in. wide.

Library table with finely marked rosewood veneers, 58in. long, circa 1840.

Edwards and Roberts fiddle-back mahogany Carlton House writing desk, circa 1900, 3ft.9in.

Victorian mahogany writing table on turned and tapered legs.

Louis XV style rosewood bonheur du jour.

Rosewood writing table, circa 1900, 32 x 24in.

Late 18th century French carved oak bonheur du jour, 40in. wide.

George III satinwood bonheur du jour on square tapering legs, 2ft.3in. wide.

Louis XIV floral marquetrey bureau-plat.

Good bamboo writing desk.

Art Nouveau mahogany writing table with drawer.

TEAPOYS

Victorian mahogany teapoy on a shaped platform base with scroll feet.

Regency simulated rosewood teapoy, lid inlaid with cut brass scrolling, 15in. wide.

William IV mahogany teapoy with octagonal hinged top, 14in. wide.

A Victorian mahogany teapoy on a carved base.

Regency mahogany teapoy with ebony inlay, 29½in. high, circa 1810.

George III satinwood teapoy on splay feet with brass cup castors.

Georgian period teapoy in mahogany, 20in. wide, circa 1825.

Early 19th century rosewood teapoy on platform base with vase feet.

TORCHERES

One of a pair of 18th century gilded torcheres, 45in. high.

One of a pair of oak Solomonic torcheres, 75in. high.

William and Mary walnut candle stand, late 17th century, 3ft.3in. high.

One of a pair of George III mahogany torcheres, 38¾in. high.

TOWEL RAILS

Victorian mahogany towel rail on twist supports.

Edwardian oak towel rail with spiral supports.

UMBRELLA STANDS

20th century oak hall stand.

20th century oak umbrella stand.

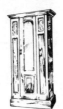

Late 18th century Dutch faded mahogany wardrobe, 70in. wide.

Heal's wardrobe of 1898.

Art Nouveau style oak wardrobe with mirror door.

Victorian carved oak hall wardrobe.

A mahogany breakfront wardrobe enclosed by four panel doors, 6ft. 6in. wide.

Rare painted wardrobe by Wm. Burges, 1870's, 53in. wide.

Satinwood and painted wardrobe, 97in. wide, circa 1880-90.

Wardrobe designed by Gordon Russell, circa 1930, 72in. high.

Late George III mahogany wardrobe, 4ft. 4in. wide.

An Art Nouveau marquetry oak wardrobe, 137cm. wide.

Early 1920's walnut and ivory wardrobe, designed by Leon Jallot, 183cm. high.

Solid walnut breakfront wardrobe by Peter Waals.

Georgian period mahogany wardrobe, 48in. wide, circa 1820.

A large, good quality, Victorian pine wardrobe.

Rosewood armoire, by Louis Majorelle, 103in. high.

Plum Pudding mahogany gentleman's wardrobe, 54in. wide, circa 1850.

Late 19th century walnut washstand with tiled splashback.

Victorian marble top washstand.

Victorian marble top wash stand.

Sheraton period corner toilet stand, circa 1790, 43¾in. high.

George III mahogany campaign washstand/writing desk, 28in. wide.

George III colonial padoukwood toilet table with divided hinged top, 2ft.1in. wide.

Georgian mahogany washstand.

Sheraton period mahogany toilet stand inlaid with ebony stringing, 22in. wide.

Victorian marble topped walnut washstand.

George III mahogany square toilet stand, circa 1790, 32in. high.

Victorian marble topped washstand.

Victorian mahogany washstand on turned legs.

Regency bow-fronted toilet cabinet with divided hinged top, 3ft. 7½in. wide.

A mahogany powdering stand, with two drawers and undershelf, on cabriole legs, 3ft.10in. high.

Late 19th century marble topped mahogany washstand with satinwood inlay.

19th century marquetry corner washstand.

102

Oriental three-tier hardwood display stand.

William IV rosewood whatnot with barley twist supports.

Regency whatnot with two drawers, 26½in. wide, 15in. deep, 29½in. high.

Late 19th century oak whatnot.

Carved oak square four tier whatnot with drawer in base, 1ft. 8ins.

Victorian walnut whatnot of serpentine form.

Mahogany whatnot, 1840's, 55½in. x 21in.

A Victorian walnut serpentine front three-tier whatnot with a drawer in the base, and spiral pillar supports, 1ft.11in. wide.

Victorian inlaid walnut whatnot with barley twist supports.

19th century rosewood whatnot, stencilled Taprell Holland & Son, London, 49cm. wide.

20th century oak serving trolley.

Regency period mahogany whatnot of kidney shape with brass string inlay and a pierced brass gallery.

Victorian inlaid walnut four-tier whatnot.

Victorian walnut rectangular three tier whatnot, 107cm. wide.

Papier mache and mother-of-pearl whatnot, 1840's, 52½in. high.

Late 17th century Japanese lacquer Shodana.

103

Regency mahogany open wine cooler, 28in. wide.

A Victorian oak hexagonal cellarette on six legs, 23in. high.

Early 18th century Sinhalese hardwood and ebony wine cooler, 2ft.7in. wide.

Large solid rosewood Anglo-Indian wine cooler, circa 1840, 30in. wide.

George III brass bound mahogany wine cooler with twin carrying handles, 11in. wide.

Georgian dome shaped tambour shuttered wine cooler.

George IV mahogany wine cooler, circa 1820, 2ft.5in. wide.

Early George III octagonal mahogany wine cooler with brass bands.

Late 18th century Dutch marquetry oval wine cooler, 1ft.8½in. wide.

Brass bound mahogany wine cooler.

George III mahogany wine cooler with brass liner and brass bound body, 23in. wide.

19th century Dutch marquetry wine cooler on cabriole legs, with brass carrying handles.

George III mahogany and brass bound wine cooler, 60cm. wide.

George III domed top mahogany wine cooler on square tapered legs.

Georgian oval brass bound wine cooler.

George III serpentine fronted mahogany cellarette, circa 1760, 1ft.6in. wide.

ALE GLASSES

Unusual cut ale wine glass, 7in. high, circa 1770.

Balustroid engraved ale glass with slender funnel bowl, circa 1740, 18cm. high.

Opaque twist ale glass with slender ogee bowl, circa 1770, 19.5cm. high.

Dwarf ale glass, circa 1750, 4in. high, bowl with wrythen moulding.

APOTHECARY BOXES

George III shagreen cased apothecary's chest, circa 1760.

Georgian mahogany and brass bound apothecary's box, complete with bottles.

Late Georgian mahogany apothecary's cabinet, 9½in. high.

Brass bound George III mahogany apothecary's box by Cox & Robinson.

BELLS

Late 16th century silver mounted latticinio bell, 5½in. high.

Victorian cranberry glass bell, 12in. high.

BISCUIT CONTAINERS

Victorian engraved glass biscuit jar on a plated and engraved stand with bun feet.

Late 19th century glass biscuit barrel with plated mounts.

BEAKERS

Newcastle purple and white slag glass beaker.

19th century Mary Gregory beaker depicting a young girl.

North Bohemian lithyalin flared beaker by F. Egermann, circa 1830, 13.5cm. high.

Facon de Venise flared beaker, 16th/17th century, 6in. high.

BOTTLES

Sealed wine bottle of dark brown metal, 8¼in. high, 1736.

Good red overlay Pekin glass bottle, with decoration of birds in flowering prunus trees, circa 1800, 19.1cm. high.

German enamelled pharmacy bottle, circa 1740, 9.5cm. high.

Bohemian Zwischengold bottle with silver cap, 12cm. high.

BOWLS

Victorian mauve carnival glass bowl.

English cut glass orange bowl, 12in. wide, circa 1790.

Miniature cameo glass bowl, circa 1880, 3.8cm. high.

19th century Lalique glass bowl of clear and opaque white glass, 10in. diam.

Early 18th century glass bowl, 11¼in. diam.

An Orrefors deep bowl by Edvin Ohrstrom, 18cm. diam.

Good Irish canoe fruit bowl, 14in. wide, circa 1810.

16th or 17th century Facon de Venise Latticinio shallow bowl, possibly Venetian, 13.5cm. diam.

BOXES

19th century ruby glass circular box and cover, 4in.

Late 19th century ruby glass casket, 9cm. wide.

CADDIES

Victorian purple slag glass tea caddy of sarcophagus form.

Rare Staffordshire 'enamel' tea bottle, 5½in. high, circa 1760.

CANDLESTICKS

Rare glass candlestick, circa 1710, 7½in. high.

Late 18th century free blown glass pricket candlestick, 9in. high.

Bronze and Favrile glass candlestick, by Tiffany, 8in. high.

Victorian ruby glass candlestick.

Large cut glass column with faceted stem, circa 1900, 54.5cm. high.

CANDELABRA

CARAFES

One of a pair of Lalique four-light candelabra, 9½in. high.

One of a pair of glass and gilt metal candelabra.

One of a pair of Spanish opaque white carafes, 18th century, 10¼in. high.

Ale carafe with cylindrical body and tapering neck, circa 1770, 25.5cm. high.

CAR MASCOTS

Lalique 'Dragonfly' mascot.

Lalique glass car mascot, 1920's, 14cm. wide.

Lalique glass car mascot 'The Archer', moulded in intaglio, 12.5cm. high.

Lalique frosted glass mascot, circa 1920, 17.5cm. high.

CENTREPIECES

CHAMPAGNE GLASSES

19th century cut glass and silver plated centrepiece with a glass bowl.

Large silvered metal Art Nouveau centrepiece, with a glass bowl, circa 1900, 45cm. high.

Pedestal stemmed champagne glass with double ogee bowl, circa 1745, 14.5cm. high.

Baluster champagne glass, circa 1720, 5½in. high.

CHANDELIERS

Double overlay glass chandelier by Daum Freres, 15½in. diam.

Fine glass ceiling fixture by Rene Lalique, circa 1925, 10¾in. diam.

Superb Adam style chandelier, circa 1785.

Highly coloured Belgian chandelier by Muller, 61cm. high.

CLARET JUGS

Victorian silver mounted clear glass 'Lotus' claret jug, 7¼in. high, by E. H. Stockwell, London, 1880.

Victorian cut glass claret jug with silver mount, Sheffield, 1871, 28cm. high.

An exceptionally fine Webb cameo glass claret jug.

Walker and Hall silver mounted claret jug, London, 1883, 25cm. high.

CORDIAL GLASSES

Opaque twist cordial glass, with funnel bowl, circa 1765, 14.5cm. high.

A Facon de Venise cordial glass, 17th century, 4¼in. high.

George III cordial glass, with funnel bowl.

Opaque twist cordial glass with funnel bowl, circa 1765, 17cm. high.

CRUETS

One of a pair of Georgian silver and glass condiment bottles, 1808, 7in. high.

Late 19th century four-bottle plated cruet.

Georgian cruet bottle, complete with stopper, circa 1810.

Early George II two-bottle cruet frame by Paul de Lamerie, London, 1728, 5½in. wide, 14oz.13dwt.

New England peach blown punch cup with ribbed handle, 2¼in. high.

Bottle glass beer mug with white enamel splatter.

Galle cameo glass stemmed honeycomb cup, 11.75cm. high, circa 1900.

Rare Jacobite mug, 4⅛in. high, with ribbed applied handle.

DECANTER BOXES

Travelling decanter case with glasses and decanters.

'Directore' mahogany decanter box, 19½in. high, circa 1912.

19th century rosewood travelling drinks cabinet.

Mahogany and inlaid decanter box with four cut-glass decanters, 8½in. high.

DECANTERS

19th century cut glass decanter.

Fine and very rare Giles opaque-white decanter, 11½in. high, circa 1775.

George III Waterford glass decanter, 20in. high, circa 1780.

Lalique glass decanter, 12in. high.

St. Louis decanter, 21.5cm. high, with dark blue and opaque white bands.

Victorian, green, Mary Gregory decanter.

Early 19th century ship's decanter.

Jacobite decanter, circa 1760, 10in. high.

DISHES

Webb cameo shallow circular dish, 8½in. diam.

Daum cameo glass dish, 14.5cm. wide, circa 1900.

Late 19th century gilt and enamelled glass dish.

Mid 16th century Venetian gilt and enamelled dish, 5¼in. diam.

DISHES, SWEETMEAT

Fine Anglo-Venetian sweetmeat dish, circa 1700, 3¼in. high.

Unusual sweetmeat dish, with cup-shaped bowl, 3¾in. high, circa 1720.

Cut glass sweetmeat glass, with double ogee bowl, 6in. high.

Sweetmeat dish with three base collars, 6¼in. high, circa 1730.

DRINKING GLASSES

Engraved composite stemmed water glass, circa 1745, 14cm. high.

18th century German stangenglas, 8in. high.

Biedermeier drinking glass in Bristol blue and pink with etched banded panel, 6in. high.

German puzzle glass, 11in. high.

EPERGNES

Silver epergne supporting engraved glass vase and dishes, by Elkington & Co., Birmingham, 1907, 1,457gm. of silver.

Unusual Victorian cranberry glass epergne with plated mounts, 11¾in. high.

George III four-branch epergne by Matthew Boulton, Birmingham, 1811, 8½in. high, 64oz.2dwt.

Victorian three-branch opaline glass epergne.

EWERS

A blue glass ewer ornament decorated by Mary Gregory, 43cm. high.

Central European gilt milchglas ewer, 5½in. high, circa 1740.

Victorian cut glass ewer.

Late 16th century Venetian amethyst baluster ewer, 9½in. high.

FIGURES

Pair of figures by Lalique in frosted glass, 56cm. high.

Lalique glass bracket shelf, 1930's, 26.25cm. wide.

Rare 18th century Venetian figurine, 6in. high, in opaque white glass.

Lalique opalescent glass figure 'Suzanne au Bain', 1920's, 23cm. high.

FIRING GLASSES

Masonic firing glass of drawn trumpet shape, 3¼in. high.

Scottish Jacobite opaque twist firing glass, 3½in. high.

Colour twist firing glass with small ovoid bowl, circa 1760, 4in. high.

Opaque twist firing glass set on double series twist stem, 1770, 10cm. high.

FLASKS

Colourless glass flask with spherical body, circa 3rd century A.D., 4¼in. high.

Manganese purple glass flask of cylindrical form, 3rd-4th century A.D., 4¼in. high.

Central European flask with enamelled decoration, circa 1740, 17.5cm. high.

Early flattened oviform flask, circa 1690, 5½in. high.

GOBLETS

Green goblet of bright emerald colour, plain stem on spirally-moulded foot, circa 1760, 13.5cm. high.

Large fox-hunting goblet, 7¼in. high, circa 1760.

Baluster goblet with flared funnel bowl, circa 1700, 17.5cm. high.

Late 16th century Facon de Venise goblet, 10¼in. high, possibly Venetian.

HUMPENS

Late 19th century enamelled humpen, 21.4cm. high.

17th/18th century 'Ochsenkopf' humpen with enamelled body, 6in. high.

Bohemian enamelled humpen, circa 1590, 11½in. high.

Franconian enamelled glass betrothal humpen and cover, 1615, 41cm. high.

INKSTANDS

Lalique amber glass inkwell and cover, 1920's, 15.75cm. diam.

Art Nouveau glass inkwell depicting a lizard emerging from a pond.

A Stourbridge millefiori inkwell.

A rare Tiffany inkwell depicting four frogs.

JARS

Mount Washington Royal Flemish covered jar, 7in. high.

Rare red Pekin glass covered jar, decorated in relief with a dragon among clouds, 12.5cm. high.

A large apothecary's jar, made of crude bottle glass with enamel splatter.

18th century German enamelled apothecary jar, 8¾in. high.

A Ravenscroft syllabub jug, gilt on sloping shoulders, with the label 'Honey Syllabub'.

Victorian white slag glass jug with thistle decoration.

Victorian cranberry glass jug with ridged decoration, 6½in. high.

Mary Gregory glass jug, 8in. high.

4th century A.D. pale green glass jug with strap handle, 3¾in. high.

Mid 16th century Venetian gilt and enamelled jug, 8¾in. high.

Enamelled milchglas jug, Spanish or Bohemian, circa 1780, 19.3cm. high.

Enamelled and gilt milchglas jug and cover, 25.5cm. high, circa 1770.

LAMPS

Lalique lamp in frosted glass, 1920's, 10½in. high.

Cut glass 'Gone with the Wind' lamp, signed L. Straus & Sons, 18½in. high.

Lithophane desk lamp with five panel shade, 15in. high.

Mid 18th century French lacemaker's lamp, 25.5cm. high.

Le Verre Francais cameo glass lamp with shouldered domed shaped shade, 1920's, 40.5cm. high.

Gilt bronze and Favrile glass three-light lily table lamp by Tiffany, 13in. high.

Tiffany Studio bronze table lamp, circa 1900, 63cm. high.

Tiffany spider web lamp with bronze baluster base.

LAMP SHADES

Yellow rose bush leaded glass hanging lamp by Tiffany, 24¾in. diam.

Victorian oil lamp shade of pink glass.

Daum cameo glass lampshade, 31cm. diam, circa 1900.

19th century Lithophane lamp shade on brass frame, 7¼in.

LIQUEUR SETS

Decanter and six glasses in stand, circa 1840.

Etched liqueur service in glass, 1930's.

Glass decanter and six glasses with silver mounts and silver overlay, circa 1920.

19th century Bohemian gilt drinking set, jug 33.5cm. high.

LUSTRES

One of a pair of gilt green glass lustres, circa 1850, 31cm. high.

One of a pair of Bohemian overlay glass lustres, with cranberry glass body, 25cm. high.

One of a pair of ruby glass lustres with floral decoration and cut glass drops.

One of a pair of ruby glass double lustres, about 1880.

MATCH-HOLDERS

Small Victorian glass shoe match-holder.

A Daum match-holder of rectangular form, the pale blue frosted glass body enamelled with an Alpine scene, 4cm. high.

MEAD GLASSES

A baluster mead glass with an incurved cup-shaped bowl, circa 1710.

Rare mead glass, 4¾in. high, circa 1700.

114

Pair of Walter pate-de-verre bookends, 1920's, 17cm. high.

Coffee and cream glass centrepiece by Webb, 10¼in. diam.

One of a pair of glass butter coolers, covers and stands, 7in., circa 1790.

Central European opaque opaline globular teapot and cover, mid 18th century, 16cm. wide.

Large Lalique frosted glass figure of a pigeon, 14.5cm. high, 1930's.

One of a pair of large cut urns and covers, 12½in. high, circa 1790.

Rare ormolu mounted cameo glass wall flowerbowl, 13in. diam.

Pale green Roman glass vessel in the form of a bucket, 13.7cm. high.

One of a pair of St. Louis fruit door handles, 2in. diam.

One of a rare pair of 18th century enamelled opaque white tureens, 4½in. high.

Pedestal stemmed stand, circa 1745, 12.5cm. high.

A Tassie glass paste portrait medallion on frosted glass over blue paper, 4¾in.

Glass vessel, possibly Roman, 2nd century A.D., 8¾in. high.

Dated St. Louis pen-holder, 1973, 13.6cm. high, set on a paperweight base.

16th century Italian verre eglomise picture, 4¼ x 3¼in.

Bohemian rose water sprinkler, circa 1850, 30.5cm. high.

PAPERWEIGHTS

St. Louis marbrie salamander weight, 8.5cm. high.

St. Louis double clematis weight, 7.5cm. diam.

Rare New England glass fruit weight, 3½in. wide.

Clichy miniature posy weight, 1¾in. diam.

Rare, Clichy convolvus weight, 3in. diam.

Lalique glass frog paperweight, 6.1cm. high, circa 1930.

St. Louis carpet-ground paperweight, 6cm. diam.

Rare, St. Louis magnum crown paperweight, 4in. diam.

PIPES

Nailsea pink and white pipe, 12in. long.

Rosewater pipe with wicker overlaid glass stem.

PITCHERS

Cased wheeling peach blown pitcher, 5¼in. high.

Galle carved glass pitcher in smoked glass, 1890's, 15.5cm. long.

PLAQUES

Sulphide glass cameo plaque of General Lafayette, 8.5cm. wide.

Cameo glass plaque by George Woodhall, circa 1885.

A carved cameo amber glass plaque by G. Woodhall, 16.5cm. high.

Baccarat sulphide glass cameo plaque of Charles X, 10cm. long.

116

Victorian plate commemorating Gladstone.

Venetian diamond engraved Latticinio plate, late 16th century, 16.5cm. diam.

19th century light blue slag glass plate with basket weave edge.

Late Victorian frosted pressed glass plate, 8in. diameter.

POTS

A small pressed blue glass Victorian dressing table bowl and cover, 3in. diam.

Daum etched and applied cameo glass pot and cover, 12.5cm. high, circa 1910.

Lithyalin pounce-pot with pewter mount, 2¾in. high.

Unusual Pekin glass brushpot, thinly cased in red, engraved mark of Qianlong, 17.5cm. high.

RATAFIA GLASSES

Ratafia glass with a narrow, straight sided funnel bowl moulded to two thirds of its height, circa 1745.

Rare Jacobite opaque twist ratafia glass with ogee bowl, circa 1765, 18cm. high.

ROEMERS

17th century Rhenish roemer of light green metal, 14cm. high.

17th century Netherlandish green tinted roemer with cup-shaped bowl, 20.5cm. high.

RUMMERS

Large engraved rummer, early 19th century, 8¼in. high.

Battle of the Boyne commemorative rummer, 1690, 6in. high.

Sunderland bridge rummer, 6½in. high, circa 1820.

One of a pair of engraved masonic rummers, 6¼in. high, circa 1820.

SCENT BOTTLES

Guerlain 'Mitsouko' glass bottle and stopper.

Webb double overlay globular scent bottle and silver screw cover, 4in. high.

Decorated clear glass perfume bottle and stopper, 13.75cm. high.

Daum scent bottle and stopper, 5in. high, signed.

Delvaux enamelled scent bottle and stopper, 1920's, 11.25cm. high.

Moulded glass perfume bottle and stopper, 12cm. high, 1920's.

Rare sulphide scent bottle of flattened circular form, 7cm. diam.

Modernist glass bottle and stopper, circa 1930, 26cm. high.

SNUFF BOTTLES

Black overlay glass bottle with quartz stopper.

Chinese opaque milk-white overlay glass snuff bottle, of blue and red overlay, with agate stopper.

Chinese opaque white glass overlay snuff bottle, red overlay, with coral glass and pearl stopper.

Red overlay glass bottle with jade stopper.

Interior-painted rock crystal snuff bottle and coral stopper, 2¾in. high.

Rare enamelled glass snuff bottle by Ku Yueh Hsuan.

Late 19th century interior painted glass snuff bottle.

Interior-painted snuff bottle by Ten Yu-t'ien.

118

TANKARDS

Central European enamelled milchglas miniature tankard, 3¼in. high, circa 1750.

Large glass tankard with scalloped foot, 6in. high, circa 1750.

Ruby glass tankard with silver hinged cover, 8in. high.

Central European enamelled tankard and cover, circa 1750, 24cm. high.

TANTALUS

Plated tantalus frame with two decanters.

Oak decanter box, circa 1880, with Bramah lock, 13¾in. wide.

TAPERSTICKS

Pedestal stemmed taperstick, 5½in. high, circa 1730.

A rare taperstick, the nozzle set on inverted baluster air twist stem, 6½in. high.

TAZZAS

Venetian filigree tazza, circa 1600, 6¾in. diam.

17th century Venetian tazza, 2in. high, 6¼in. diam.

Late 16th century Facon de Venise enamelled glass tazza, 5.9in. high.

17th century Venetian tazza, 8in. diam.

TUMBLERS

Baccarat armorial tumbler with enamelled coat of arms, 9.5cm. high.

Engraved glass tumbler, 4¾in. high, circa 1790.

Venetian enamelled tumbler, 18th century, 4½in. high.

Bohemian tumbler engraved with cupids and allegorial scenes, circa 1730, 10.2cm. high.

VASES

One of a pair of flower encrusted bottle vases.

18th century pale blue ground bottle vase, 8¾in. high.

One of a pair of portrait overlay green glass vases, circa 1850, 33.8cm. high.

Very rare Staffordshire opaque white enamelled glass vase, 5in. high, circa 1760.

An escalier de cristal ormolu mounted cameo vase, 16.5cm. high.

One of a pair of Art Nouveau silver overlay blue vases.

Very rare miniature opaque white globular vase, 2½in. high, circa 1770.

Pate de verre small oviform vase, 3¼in. diam.

ARGY ROUSSEAU

Argy Rousseau pate de cristal vase, 14.75cm. high, 1920's.

Pate de cristal Argy Rousseau vase, 10in. high.

BOHEMIAN

One of a pair of Bohemian ruby overlay glass vases, 10in. high.

One of a pair of Bohemian overlay trumpet shaped vases.

DAUM

Daum etched, carved and enamelled glass vase, circa 1900, 13.5cm. high.

Daum cameo glass vase of teardrop form, 30.25cm. high, circa 1900.

Signed Daum Nancy vase in orange, cream and green, 6½in. high.

Daum etched and gilt 'vase pariant', circa 1900, 26cm. high.

Mounted Galle cameo glass vase, circa 1890's, 7.75cm. high.

Galle, etched and carved cameo glass vase, 19.5cm. high, circa 1900.

Small Galle cameo glass vase, 7.75cm. high, circa 1900.

A superb and very rare glass vase, by Emile Galle, 11¼in. high.

LALIQUE

Lalique frosted glass vase, relief moulded, 1930's, 13.5cm. high.

Heavy Lalique frosted glass vase, 1930's, 25.5cm. high.

Good Lalique 'grasshopper' vase, 27cm. high, 1920's.

Heavy Lalique cylindrical glass vase, 22.5cm. high, 1920's.

LEGRAS

LOETZ

A Legras cameo glass vase of quatrefoil shape, the frosted glass body overlaid in purple, 13cm. high.

Legras etched and internally decorated glass vase, 39cm. high, 1920's.

Loetz iridescent glass vase, 18.5cm. high, circa 1900.

One of a pair of Loetz iridescent vases.

NAMED

Orrefors engraved glass vase, 18.75cm. high, 1940's.

A Brocard enamelled cylindrical vase with stylised cornflower sprays, 16.5cm. high.

Signed Sabino vase, circa 1920, with fish motif, 8in. high.

J. F. Christy oviform vase designed by Richard Redgrave, 1847, 15cm. high.

121

MULLER FRERES

Muller Freres cameo glass vase, circa 1900, 19.5cm. high.

Large Muller Freres cameo glass landscape vase, circa 1900, 55cm. high.

STOURBRIDGE

Late 19th century vase attributed to Joshua Hodgetts, Stourbridge, white on amethyst glass, 27.5cm. high.

WEBB

Cameo glass vase by Thos. Webb & Sons, 10.8cm. high.

WINDOWS

15th century English stained glass roundel, 4½in. diam.

Stourbridge cameo glass vase, 5in. high, central band with turquoise 'jewelling'.

Webb three colour cameo glass vase.

French stained glass panel showing the Risen Christ, dated 1542, 66 x 56cm.

PEKIN

Pekin overlay glass vase of bottle form from the Qianlong period.

TIFFANY

Tiffany Favrile iridescent millefiori oviform vase, 6in. high.

Late 19th century Webb cameo glass vase, 9.5cm. high.

Early 20th century stained glass window depicting a peacock, 22in. high.

Well carved Imperial yellow Pekin glass vase of beaker form carved with blossom, 20.5cm. high.

A rare Jack-in-the-Pulpit Tiffany peacock iridescent glass vase, 1900.

Rare early 20th century Webb 'rock crystal' engraved vase by Wm. Fritsche, 25cm. high.

German or Swiss stained glass panel showing a married couple, dated 1597, 33 x 24cm.

German Royal commemorative glass, engraved with a horseman.

Fine, large gilt wine glass, circa 1760, 7½in. high.

Baluster wine glass with funnel bowl, circa 1710, 14cm. high.

Incised twist bright emerald green wine glass, 1750, 13.3cm. high.

Engraved Hanoverian wine glass, 6½in. high, circa 1740.

Facet stemmed wine glass, with ogee bowl, cut in the style of James Giles, circa 1780, 15cm. high.

Engraved colour twist wine glass in the Jacobite taste, circa 1770, 14.5cm. high.

Unusual Lynn wine glass, 5¾in. high, circa 1750.

17th century Facon de Venise wine glass, 6¼in. high.

Multi-knopped air twist wine glass, circa 1750, 6¼in. high.

Very rare wine glass, circa 1740, 7½in. high.

Dutch engraved whaling glass, 7¼in. high, circa 1750.

Beilby enamelled glass with bell bowl, 6½in. high, circa 1765.

Facon de Venise winged wine glass, Low Countries, 17th century, 18cm. high.

Canary twist wine glass with hammer moulded bowl, circa 1760, 6in. high.

A magnificent Beilby armorial goblet inscribed 'W. Beilby Jr.', dated 1762, 8¾in. high.

123

Barograph by Short and Mason.

Late 19th century sextant with brass frame.

Late 19th century American J.H. Bunnell & Co., brass recording telegraph.

Early 19th century set of drawing instruments, 5in. long.

Bronze sundial of horizontal pedestal type.

Sheraton mahogany terrestial globe, circa 1825, 18in. high.

Two-day marine chronometer by Breguet et Cie, dial 8cm. diam.

Early Culpeper microscope, 14in. high, with drawer of objectives and slides.

Unusual jockey's scale, circa 1880, with mahogany seat.

Dollands chest type brass monocular microscope, circa 1840.

Good brass theodolite, 350mm. high.

Danish magneto desk telephone, circa 1920, 1ft.1in. high.

Unusual London Stereoscopic Co. double stereoscopic viewer, circa 1880, 1ft.8in. high.

Early 20th century orrery, 3ft.5in. wide, with sectioned diagram.

19th century brass astronomical telescope on a steel stand by Jas. Parker

Ship's Bridge Telegraph in brass, 105cm. high, signed 'Bloctube Controls'.

Black-lacquered metal
coal bin.

A pair of German iron candlesticks, circa 1910, 21cm.
high.

Iron tsuba, 7.7cm., signed
Sunagawa Masayoshi.

Late 17th century German
iron casket, 8in. long.

IVORY

Early 17th century
South German ivory
relief, 2¾in. high.

Early 18th century Italian
ivory oval plaque, 4¼in.
long.

Harpoon support in walrus
ivory.

Late 19th century
ivory tusk vase,
25.5cm. high.

South German ivory group,
4½in. high, circa 1600.

18th century Dieppe car-
ved ivory group, 3½in. high.

German silver coloured
metal and ivory tankard,
8½in. high.

19th century Japanese
carved ivory figure.

Carved ivory figure
of Hsi Wang Mu,
34cm. high, Chinese,
circa 1900.

Japanese ivory Okimono sec-
tional group, signed Kyokumei,
late 19th century, 7in. high.

Japanese carved ivory sec-
tional takarabune, 52cm. long.

Carved ivory female head
by Julien Dillens, 55cm.
high, circa 1900.

125

JADE

Pale grey jade hexagonal vase, 4¼in. high.

Qianlong mottled white jade koro and cover, 6¾in. wide.

Mottled white and brown jade bottle.

18th century Chinese celadon jade bowl, 23.5cm. wide.

LEAD

18th century lead cistern, dated 1764, 39in. wide.

Naja by Jean Dunand in patinated lead.

MARBLE

Late 18th century neoclassic Italian marble trough, 26¾in. wide.

17th century North Italian marble negro head, 14in. high.

MIRRORS

Guernardeau patinated metal Art Nouveau mirror frame, circa 1900, 41.5cm. high.

Good George II parcel gilt walnut mirror, 2ft.3in. wide.

Early George III giltwood mirror, 47¾in. high.

Walnut cheval mirror, 1850's, 78in. high.

MONEY BANKS

Late 19th century American Punch and Judy money box, 7½in. high.

20th century English cast iron Artillery bank in the form of a cannon which fires coins into a pill box.

MUSICAL BOXES

Late 19th century symphonium disc musical box, 1ft.10in. wide.

Columbia type BVT graphophone, circa 1908, American.

126

Fine late William and Mary posset pot in pewter, 9½in. wide, circa 1695.

Rare lidless pewter tavern pot, by IG, 5in. high, circa 1720-30.

French lidded cylindrical measure, 19th century, 11in. high.

Deep-welled 'Mount Edgecumbe' bowl with broad rim, 14in. diam., circa 1640.

Polished pewter water jug with cane handle by Liberty & Co., circa 1905.

Rare, William & Mary pewter candlestick, 6½in. high, circa 1690.

Late 18th century German flask, 8¾in. high, in pewter.

Early Georgian pewter tankard by Richard Going, 6½in. high, circa 1725.

PIANOS

Upright oak Broadwood 'Manxman' piano, circa 1900, 56½in. wide.

Strohmenger painted satinwood baby grand piano and duet stool.

Upright iron framed piano by John Brinsmead, London.

20th century red lacquer chinoiserie baby grand piano by Bluthner.

SHIBAYAMA

Japanese carved Shibayama and ivory figure, circa 1900, 15.5cm. high.

Japanese Shibayama and silver filigree tray, circa 1900, 30cm. wide.

Fine quality Japanese Shibayama incense burner.

Shibayama box and cover, signed Masasada, 3¼in. wide.

BASKETS
CAKE

A fine pierced silver cake basket by Paul de Lamerie, 1773, 14in., 19½oz. 1731.

George III silver cake basket by Wm. Tuite, London, 1773, 14in., 19½oz.

George III oval shaped cake basket, 14¼in. wide, by Chawner & Emes, London, 1796, 21oz.11dwt.

Regency oblong cake basket by Benjamin and James Smith, 1810, 47oz., 13¼in. long.

SUGAR

Silver sugar basket by Peter and Anne Bateman, 4½oz.

Small George III pierced silver basket by Robt. Hennell, 1787, 4oz.

Small George III basket by Hester Bateman, London, 1789, 3in. wide.

Early 19th century German oval sugar vase on foot, 7oz.10dwt.

SWEETMEAT

George III silver gilt metal oval sweetmeat basket, 6¾in. wide, by Vere & Lutwyche, London, 1767, 6oz.5dwt.

George III boat-shaped sweetmeat basket, 6in. wide, by Henry Chawner, London, 1791, 8oz.3dwt.

George III octagonal silver footed sweetmeat basket, London, 1794, by Robt. Hennell.

George III boat-shaped silver sweetmeat basket, by Peter, Anne and William Bateman.

BEAKERS

17th century German silver gilt beaker, 2½in. high, 2oz.18dwt.

One of a matching pair of silver gilt beakers by E. Barnard & Sons, London, 1862-68, 12.2cm. high, 748gm.

Early 18th century German silver gilt beaker by Esajas Busch, Augsburg, 1705, 3¼in. high, 4oz.12dwt.

Silver gilt and niello beaker, by E. C., Moscow, 1846, 6.7cm. high.

18th century Dutch table bell, 4¼in. high, by Jan Bot, Amsterdam, 1748, 8oz.18dwt.

Table bell by Elkington & Co. Ltd., Birmingham, 1890, 11.5cm. high.

George IV coronation bell, 5in. high, by T. Phipps & E. Robinson, London, 1820, 6oz. 19dwt.

Good Dutch silver gilt bell by Cornelis de Haan, The Hague, 1775, 5½in. high, 10oz.10dwt.

BISCUIT CONTAINERS

Circular biscuit barrel, 5½in. high, London, 1931, 17oz.6dwt.

Art Nouveau lantern style biscuitiere with glass liner, 1900.

E.P.N.S. oak biscuit barrel with ceramic lining, circa 1910.

George III circular biscuit barrel, 6¾in. high, by Solomon Hougham, London, 1801, 7oz.14dwt.

BOWLS

Late 17th century Dutch brandy bowl, by Thos. Sibrand Hicht, Dokkum, 1684, 8½in. wide, 5oz. 14dwt.

One of a pair of ornate Victorian silver bowls, 7in. diameter, London, 1899, 23oz.

Chinese export silver bowl, circa 1880.

George III Scottish circular bowl, by R. Gray & Son, Edinburgh, 1811, 8oz.8dwt., 5in. diam.

Jensen silver bowl and spoon, 10cm. high, circa 1947.

18th century Dutch tub-shaped covered bowl, 3½in. diam., by Marcelis de Haan, The Hague, 6oz. 5dwt.

Early Charles II bleeding bowl, 5½in. diam., London, 1664, 7oz.6dwt.

18th century silver gilt circular bowl and stand, 63oz.3dwt.

BOWLS
MONTEITH

William III Monteith bowl, by Robert Timbrell, London, 1698, 57oz.4dwt., 11in. diam.

Large sterling silver Monteith bowl with repousse decoration, with gilded lining, by Charles Harris, London, 1876.

William III Monteith bowl, by Robert Peake, London, 1700, 50oz. 10dwt., 11in. diam.

Large, late 18th century plated Sheffield Monteith bowl, 12in. high.

PUNCH

Silver punch bowl by William Davie, Edinburgh, 1785, 64oz.

Victorian punch bowl.

Rare early American silver punch bowl, by John Coney.

Large Victorian punch bowl, Birmingham, 1890, 14in. diameter.

ROSE

Victorian silver rosebowl, London, 1895, by Child & Child.

Mappin & Webb Ltd., circular three-handled rosebowl, London, 1918, 30.4cm. diam.

Indian silver rosebowl on stand.

Circular silver rosebowl, by Omar Ramsden, 1935, 70oz.18dwt., 11¾in. wide.

SUGAR

Early 19th century Russian sugar bowl, 6½in. wide, 1805, 17oz.17dwt.

Squat silver sugar bowl, by Abraham Pootholt and Jan van Giffen, 1779, 4in. high.

Liberty & Co. silver sugar basin and tongs, Birmingham, circa 1903-06, 4cm. high.

George II covered sugar bowl, 4½in. high, by Francis Crump, London, 1750, 9oz.18dwt.

Large George IV brandy saucepan and cover by James Scott, Dublin, 1824, 5½in. high, 21oz. 10dwt.

George III silver saucepan, 4in. high, by F. Knopfell, London, 1768, 19oz.9dwt.

Early George III brandy saucepan, 4½in. high, by Benjamin Brewood II, London, 1766, 19oz.1dwt.

George I brandy saucepan, 2¼in. high, by William Fleming, London, 1720, 5oz.17dwt.

BUCKLES

Silver belt buckle, 1892, 3¼in. long.

A Liberty silver and enamel buckle in the manner of Jessie M. King, Birmingham, 1908.

Rectangular Art Nouveau silver buckle, London, 1902, 5.5cm. wide.

Art Nouveau belt buckle, 7.75cm. wide, probably American, circa 1900.

CANDELABRA

One of a pair of Sheffield plated three-light candelabra.

Stylish German six-light candelabrum, circa 1910, 57cm. high, in silver coloured metal.

One of two Victorian seven-light candelabra, 31½in. high, by Messrs. Barnard, 369oz.

One of a pair of Goldsmiths & Silversmiths Co., silver four-light candelabra, in 18th century style, 1902, 40.5cm. high.

One of a pair of George III candelabra, 15¾in. high, by John Winter & Co., Sheffield, 1773.

One of a pair of 18th century German candelabra, Augsburg, 1793-95, 17in. high, 70oz.12dwt.

One of a pair of 18th century German two-light candelabra, circa 1785, 56oz.2dwt., 14in. high.

One of a pair of silver gilt two-light candelabra, by J. Scofield, 1783, 16½in. high

CANDLESTICKS

One of a pair of William and Mary candlesticks, by F.S.S., London, 1690, 4½in. high, 16oz.8dwt.

One of a pair of silver candlesticks, London, 1894.

One of a pair of Martin Hall & Co. Ltd. table candlesticks, 23.5cm. high, London, 1893.

One of a pair of Edward Barnard & Sons table candlesticks, in the manner of Rundell, Bridge & Rundell, 1918, 2,360gm.

One of a pair of Wm. Hutton & Sons Ltd. table candlesticks, 28.5cm. high, London, 1910.

One of a set of four George III table candlesticks, by T. & J. Settle, Sheffield, 1815, 13½in. high.

One of four George II table candlesticks, by Paul de Lamerie, 6½in. high, London, 1731, 65oz.15dwt.

One of a pair of Dutch silver table candlesticks, Delft, 1677, 8½in. high, 29oz.

One of a set of four George II table candlesticks, by J. Cafe, 1750-52, 226oz., 10½in. high.

One of a pair of James Dixon & Sons large silver candlesticks, Sheffield, 1918, 30.5cm. high.

CARD CASES

Edwardian engine turned silver card case, Birmingham, 1905, 4in. tall.

Victorian tortoiseshell card case with silver string inlay, 4in. tall.

Oriental silver card case with embossed floral design, 4in. tall.

Victorian parcel gilt woman's visiting card case by Edward Smith, Birmingham, 1850.

CASKETS

German silver rectangular casket, late 19th/early 20th century, 26.6cm. long, 1,116gm.

17th century Dutch marriage casket, 3in. wide, circa 1630, 3oz.17dwt.

George IV oblong commemorative casket, 8¾in. wide, by Joseph Angell, London, 1823, 29oz.14dwt.

An electroplated electrotype jewel casket, 10½in. long, by Alexandre Tahan, circa 1854.

CASTERS

George I octagonal caster, by Glover Johnson, London, 1717. 6oz.13dwt.

Queen Anne caster, London, 1713, by Charles Adams, 6½in. high, 7oz.

Queen Anne cylindrical caster with pierced lid, 6½in. high, 6oz.17dwt.

Silver sugar caster, 7in. high, London, 1934, 7oz. 5dwt.

CENTREPIECES

George V table centrepiece with pierced and moulded decorations, 14in. high.

Victorian centrepiece by Stephen Smith, 1874, 172oz., 15¼in. high.

WMF Art Nouveau German silver centrepiece, 1925, 30in. high.

Large Jensen silver coupe, London, 1922, 19.75cm. high.

CHALICES

18th century Italian chalice and paten, by Giovanni Valadier, Rome, 10¼in. high, circa 1775, 24oz.10dwt.

Rare German gilt metal chalice, by Marcus Purman, 1608, 12.4cm. high.

Elizabeth I chalice and cover, 1570, 7in. high, 8oz. 16dwt.

Rare Elizabethan provincial chalice, 5¾in. high, Norwich, 1567, 6oz.18dwt.

CHAMBERSTICKS

Victorian taperstick, 4¼in. diam., by Charles Fox, 1838, 4oz.11dwt.

George II chamber candlestick, by Elizabeth Godfrey, London, 1750, 6in. high, 14oz.

George III chamber candlestick by R. & S. Hennell, London, 1802, 10oz., 5¼in. diameter.

James II chamber candlestick, 3½in. diam., 2oz., maker's mark T.E.

133

CHOCOLATE POTS

Rare George III baluster chocolate pot, by R. Williams, Dublin, circa 1770, 10in. high, 36oz.

Queen Anne tapered cylindrical chocolate pot, by R. Timbrell and J. Bell, London, 1711, 25oz.11dwt., 10in. high.

18th century German chocolate pot, 7¼in. high, by Johann Heinrich Menzel, Augsburg, circa 1735, 15oz.1dwt.

Short spouted chocolate pot, by David Willaume, Jnr., 1744, 10¼in. high, 45oz.10dwt., with wickerwork handle.

CIGARETTE CASES

Silver and enamel cigarette case, 1925, 8.4cm. high.

Russian silver cigarette case enamelled in dark blue, orange, green and claret.

Continental rectangular cigarette case, 3½in. high.

Silver Art Nouveau cigarette case, Birmingham, 1905, 9cm. high.

CLARET JUGS

John Foligno claret jug, London, 1806.

Cut glass and silver claret jug, complete with stopper, 1902.

Saunders & Shepherd silver mounted glass claret jug, London, 1895, 20.4cm. high.

Late 19th century silver mounted cut glass claret jug.

COASTERS

One of a pair of William IV wine coasters, 5¾in. diam.

One of four Russian shaped circular wine coasters by Nichols & Plinke, 1859.

One of a set of four George III circular pierced coasters, by R. Hennell, 12.5cm. diam.

One of a pair of George IV wine coasters by J. Crouch and W. Reid, London, 1821, 6¼in. diam.

134

Silver coffee pot by S. Hennell, London, 1841, 34oz.

Silver gilt coffee pot, 1823, on a heater stand, 8in. high, by Wm. Eley.

Fine cylindrical silver chocolate pot, 1725, 9in. high, 26oz.10dwt., made by Joseph Clare.

A magnificent George II silver coffee pot, by de Lamerie, made in 1738.

18th century Swiss coffee pot, 8¼in. high, Geneva, circa 1770, 16oz.

George III baluster coffee pot, by Benjamin Gignac, London, 1767, 11¼in. high, 31oz.15dwt.

Side-handled coffee pot, by David Tanqueray, 9½in. high, 33oz.10dwt.

Vase-shaped silver coffee pot, by Daniel Smith and Robert Sharp, 1776, 11in. high, 24oz.

CREAM BOATS

George II Scottish cream-boat, by John Main, Edinburgh, 1739, 6½in. wide, 7oz.14dwt.

Irish George III silver creamboat, Dublin 1811.

George II creamboat, 5¼in., by William Cripps, London, 1743, 6oz.2dwt.

George III silver creamboat, by Wm. Harrison, 1763.

CRUETS

George III oblong silver gilt egg cruet by John Emes, London, 1806, 37oz.6dwt., 7¼in. wide.

Jensen silver cruet, circa 1950-55.

George III cruet frame, by Paul Storr, 11½in. high, 31oz.1dwt., with six cut glass bottles.

George III oval cruet frame and bottles, by Robert and David Hennell, London, 1799.

CUPS

Edwardian silver double-handled prize cup, 5oz. 5dwt.

Coconut cup with 17th century silver mounts, bearing an inscription, 3½in. diam.

Silver loving cup, by Hester Bateman, circa 1789.

Commonwealth two-handled cup and cover, marked on base and lid, maker's mark A. F. in a shaped shield, London, 1653.

George II silver gilt two-handled cup and cover, by John Le Sage, London, 1736, 24oz.1dwt., 8¼in. high.

Standing cup, by Omar Ramsden, 7¼in. high, London, 1938, 24oz. 15dwt.

Wm. Hutton & Sons Ltd., twin-handled silver cup, 28cm. high, London, 1902.

Charles S. Harris & Son Ltd., two-handled cup and cover, London, 1904, 30.7cm. high, 1,924gm.

CAUDLE

Commonwealth silver gilt caudle cup and cover, by N. Wollaston, London, 1656, 4½in. high, 13oz.12dwt.

Charles II caudle cup and cover, by Garthorne, London, 1682, 22oz.6dwt., 6½in. high.

CHRISTENING

18th century Channel Islands christening cup, 2¾in. high.

Silver Victorian christening cup, by J. Angel, 1851, 4oz.

STIRRUP

Late 18th century fox mask stirrup cup.

One of a pair of George III parcel gilt stirrup cups, by John Carter, London, 1773.

TUMBLER

18th century Norwegian parcel gilt tumbler cup, 1oz.9dwt., 1¾in. high.

One of a set of three early 18th century parcel gilt tumbler cups, circa 1700, 9oz.2dwt.

136

James I silver gilt wine cup, 8in. high, London, 1610, 10oz.12dwt.

One of a pair of George III Scottish wine cups, 7in. high, Edinburgh, 1805, 22oz.16dwt.

George III wine cup, 6in. high, by Hester Bateman, London, 1787, 5oz. 19dwt.

Unusual Charles II wine cup, circa 1675, 3½in. high, 2oz.6dwt.

DISHES

Silver chafing dish with Belgian hall marks, 1772.

18th century East European parcel gilt dish and cover, 10¾in. diam. 22oz.5dwt.

Victorian Irish potato dish, Dublin, 1896, 10in. diam., 24oz.

Hukin & Heath silver sweetmeat dish, 14cm. high, London, 1881.

17th century Dutch silver embossed dish, maker's mark H.N., Hague, 1666, 82oz.

WMF silvered metal dish, circa 1900, 17.5cm. high.

One of a pair of George I silver gilt strawberry dishes, 8½in. diam., London, 1719, 24oz.18dwt.

Breakfast dish and cover in Sheffield Plate, about 1820.

ENTREE

One of a pair of Victorian, shaped oval entree dishes and covers by R. Garrard, 1848, 13½in. long, 120oz.

George III entree dish and cover, 12¼in. wide, by J. Edwards, London, 41oz. 14dwt.

One of a set of four George IV octagonal entree dishes and covers, 10¾in. wide, by Wm. Eley, London, 1827, 205oz.16dwt.

George III silver oblong entree dish and cover by Paul Storr, London, 1808, 63oz.5dwt.

DISHES
FRUIT

Boat-shaped silver openwork fruit dish by Mappin & Webb, Sheffield, 1913, 752gm.

George IV oval fruit dish, 30in. wide, by Marshall & Sons, Edinburgh, 151oz.

Italian two-handled shaped oval fruit dish, 20th century, 48cm. wide, 1,271gm.

MEAT

George III oval meat dish, 16in. wide, by William Burwash, London, 1817, 49oz.10dwt.

Kayserzinn meat dish and cover, 55cm. long, circa 1900.

One of a pair of George II oval meat dishes, by Simon Jouet, 1759, 18in. long, 124oz.

SWEETMEAT

A very fine silver sweetmeat box, maker's mark B.B. with a crescent below, London, 1676, 18.4cm., 21oz.12dwt.

Charles I circular shaped sweetmeat dish, 6¾in. diam., London, 1638, 4oz.16dwt.

17th century German sweetmeat dish, Augsburg, circa 1675, 5¼in. wide, 2oz.9dwt.

German oval sweetmeat dish, circa 1685, 2oz. 10dwt., 5in. wide.

VEGETABLE

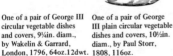

One of a pair of George III circular vegetable dishes and covers, 9¼in. diam., by Wakelin & Garrard, London, 1796, 64oz.12dwt.

One of a pair of George III plain circular vegetable dishes and covers, 10½in. diam., by Paul Storr, 1808, 116oz.

One of a pair of Victorian silver vegetable dishes on warming stands.

George III circular vegetable dish and cover, by Paul Storr, London, 1796, 107oz. 1dwt., 12¾in. diam.

Silver plated epergne, circa 1825, 15½in. high.

George III epergne, by Emick Romer, London, 1770, 91oz. 19dwt., 17¼in. high.

Silver epergne by A. H., London, 1864.

George III epergne, 15¼in. high, by Thos. Pitts, London, 1774, 129oz.12dwt.

EWERS

17th century Italian ewer, Naples, 24oz.10dwt., 9in. high.

Russian silver ewer and basin, St. Petersburg, 1841.

17th century helmet-shaped ewer, 7¼in. high, 21oz.4dwt.

American silver flask-shaped wine ewer and tray by Gorham Mfg. Co., Providence, R. I. 1882, 1,027gm.

FISH SERVERS

Silver fish trowel by Richard Williams, 1770, 13in. long.

Pair of late 19th century fish servers with bone handles, circa 1880.

18th century Dutch serving slice, 15¼in. long, by Wm. Pont, Amsterdam, 1772, 6oz.14dwt.

FLAGONS

George IV cylindrical flagon by R. Emes and E. Barnard, 1826, 61oz.

Victorian silver flagon, 11in. high, by John Mitchell, Glasgow, 1854, 39oz.16dwt.

Silver replica of a late 17th century flagon, by Lambert & Co., London, 1908, 1,563gm.

One of two late 17th century small flagons, 9in. high, 56oz.7dwt.

One of ten French dessert services, circa 1825.

Three pieces of silver, by Charles Rennie Mackintosh.

Dutch travelling knife, fork and spoon set, circa 1700.

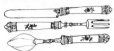

Pair of plated salad servers made in 1920's.

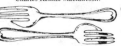

Pair of 18th century oyster forks, Old English thread.

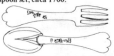

Two of six pieces of Louis XIV table silver by Louis Nicolle, circa 1687.

One of a set of twelve silver gilt spoons, made in 1592.

Rare early 17th century French two-prong fork.

Charles II silver spoon with rare boar's head finial.

George III silver caddy spoon by Samuel Pemberton, London 1807.

Guild of Handicrafts Ltd. silver butter knife, circa 1900, 13.5cm. long.

Tablespoon by Hester Bateman, London, 1766.

Part of a George III crested hour glass pattern set of table silver by Wallis & Hayne, London, 116oz.10dwt.

Part of a Reed & Barton extensive canteen of 'Francis I' pattern tableware, 301oz., circa 1949.

19th century German table silver by J.F. Brahmfeld, Hamburg, 117oz.

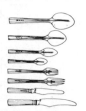

Part of forty-four pieces of table silver, by Omar Ramsden, London, 1926-38, 54oz.8dwt.

Fine Georg Jensen silver flatware service, circa 1910.

Part of a silver gilt dessert service, 1824-32, 118oz. 15dwt.

GOBLETS

HONEY POTS

SILVER

One of a pair of silver gilt German goblets, 17th century.

Late 19th century Russian cup-shaped goblet, 4¼in. high, 5oz.9dwt.

Silver gilt honey pot and matched stand, by Paul Storr, 1798, 4¾in. high, 14oz.

George III 'Skep' honey pot and stand, London, 1798-1800, 12oz.17dwt., 4¾in. high.

INKSTANDS

George II rectangular inkstand, 9¼in. wide, by William Shaw, London, 1730, 24oz.16dwt.

Two-bottle silver inkstand, by Burrage Davenport, London, 1777, 4in. long, 4oz.

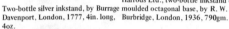

Harrods Ltd., two-bottle inkstand on moulded octagonal base, by R. W. Burbridge, London, 1936, 790gm.

Edwardian silver plated inkwell by Mappin and Webb, about 1910.

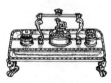

George III oblong inkstand, 8in. wide, by Susanna Barker, London, 1770, 20oz. 7dwt.

George III silver inkstand by Paul Storr, London 1803, 14¼in. wide.

JUGS

George III baluster silver jug with embossed decoration.

George IV small brandy jug on stand with burner, 7¾in. high, by J. Angell, London 1825, 16oz. 19dwt.

Silver jug, by Abraham Pootholt and Jan van Giffen, 6in. high, 1784.

Victorian 'Cellini' jug with hinged lid, 14½in. high, London 1884, 42oz.

141

JUGS
BEER

George II baluster beer jug, 8½in. high, by Thos. Coffin, Exeter, 1734, 28oz.7dwt.

George I covered beer jug, by John Edwards, London, 1719, 10in. high, 32oz. 19dwt.

Martin Hall & Co. heavy ovoid silver beer jug with armorial engraving, London, 1874, 1,711gm.

George II baluster shaped silver beer jug, by Wm. Darker, London, 1730, 25oz.

CREAM

Georgian silver cream jug, 3½oz., circa 1820.

George III silver cow creamer, 5¾in. long, by John Schuppe, 1765, 5oz.12dwt.

George II circular cream jug, by Thos. Sutton, Dublin, 1735, 3¼in. high, 4oz.10dwt.

George III helmet-shaped cream jug, 5¾in. high, London, 1793, 3oz.13dwt.

COFFEE

18th century baluster shaped silver coffee jug, 7in. high, 11.9oz.

George III coffee jug on stand, 12in. high, by Paul Storr, London 1807, 54oz. 11dwt.

George III baluster coffee jug by Wm. Bruce, London, 1814, 21oz.19dwt., 8¾in. high.

Vase-shaped fluted coffee jug, by Ambrose Boxwell, Dublin, circa 1775, 27½oz.

MILK

George III helmet-shaped milk jug, by Robert Sharp, London, 1793, 5in. high, 7oz.8dwt.

George III milk jug, by Hester Bateman, London, 1777, 6½in. high, 6oz. 12dwt.

George III Scottish provincial covered milk jug, by John Baillie, Inverness, circa 1780, 4¾in. high, 8oz.4dwt.

George II Newcastle milk jug, 4½in. high, by Wm. Whitfield, 1742, 4oz. 19dwt.

142

JUGS

HOT WATER

SILVER

A fine Hester Bateman baluster hot water jug, 1783.

William IV silver water jug, London, 1837.

George III hot water jug, by Thos. Wynn, London, 1777, 26oz., 11in. high.

Late Georgian hot water jug, London, 1831, 27½oz., 10½in. high.

WINE

Queen Anne Irish wine jug, by Thos. Boulton of Dublin, 1702.

Silver wine jug by John S. Hunt, London, 1850, 13½in. high.

George II Irish, covered jug, by Erasmus Cope, Dublin, 1736, 33oz.8dwt.

George III baluster wine jug.

KOVSCH

Superb silver Russian kovsch, probably by Maria Somenova.

Enamelled silver gilt kovsch by Carl Faberge, circa 1913, 7in. long.

19th century Russian kovsch in silver and enamel inlaid with green and red stones.

Enamelled silver kovsch by Carl Faberge, circa 1910, 2½in. long.

LADLES

One of a pair of George II Hanoverian pattern sauce ladles, by Elias Cachart, London, 1744, 5oz.5dwt.

Fluted silver punch ladle, by E. Aldridge, 1742.

Bright cut ladle, by R. Keay, Perth, 1790.

LEMON STRAINERS

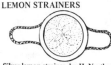

Silver lemon strainer, by H. Northcote, 1799.

George I silver lemon strainer, Francis Nelme, London, 1727.

Late 18th century, bright cut silver strainer, 10in. across.

143

MODELS

Late 19th century silver model of a bull, 72oz. 13dwt., 18¼in. overall.

One of a pair of Portuguese 19th century models of Kylins, 106oz., 14½in. high.

Crane with silver body and copper beak, circa 1900. 5¾in. high.

One of a pair of B. Neresheimer & Sohne figures of knights, Hanau, 1911, 2,795gm.

MUGS

George III silver christening mug, London, 1798, by John Emes, 3oz.

A small slightly tapering silver beer mug with scroll handle, London, 1801, 8½oz.

George III silver pint baluster mug, by John Deacon, 1769, 5in. high, 10½oz.

Charles II tapering cylindrical mug, by Jonah Kirk, London, 1683, 9oz. 8dwt., 4in. high.

MULLS

Horn snuff mull, probably Tain, circa 1837.

Scottish horn mull with silver mounts, 8¾in. long, circa 1760.

Silver mounted ram's head table snuff mull, about 1880, 13½in. high.

Scottish snuff mull, circa 1800.

MUSTARDS

Italian mustard pot and stand, Naples, 1792, stand 4½in. diam., 7oz.10dwt.

Early Victorian mustard pot by Charles Fox, London, 1837, 3in. high, 4oz.12dwt.

Charles T. and George Fox owl shaped mustard pot, 11.5cm. high, 9.9oz.

George III barrel-shaped mustard pot, by Robert and David Hennell, London, 1798, 3in. high, 3oz.13dwt.

NEFS

Continental two-masted nef on four wheels, circa 1900, 15¼in. high.

Late 19th century silver Dutch nef, 24in. long, mounted on a carriage.

Late 19th century German nef on dolphin stem, with pseudo hallmarks, 732gm.

Continental two-masted nef on four wheels, 17½in. high, dated for 1901.

NUTMEGS

Late 18th century egg-shaped nutmeg grater, by Samuel Meriton.

Silver nutmeg grater by Elkington & Co., Birmingham, 1906, 3in. long.

George III silver nutmeg grater, by Mary Hyde and John Reily, London, 1799, 2in. diam.

Georgian silver nutmeg grater, by Phipps & Robinson, London, 1788, 2¾in. high.

PAP BOATS

Georgian silver pap boat, maker's mark TE, 4¾in., 2oz.

Unmarked silver and coconut shell pap boat, circa 1760, 5in. long.

George III silver pap boat, by Rebecca Emes and Edward Barnard, 2½oz.

PEPPERS

George I cylindrical kitchen pepper, by John Hamilton, Dublin, 2½in. high, 2oz.9dwt.

Pair of silver mounted Victorian ivory pepperettes.

One of two Handicrafts Ltd. pepper casters, circa 1900, 6.5cm. high.

Gallia cruet set, 8cm. high, in silvered metal, 1920's.

145

PHOTOGRAPH FRAMES

Art Nouveau silver photograph frame, 6in. high.

Liberty & Co. silver and enamel frame, Birmingham, 1910, 27cm. high.

One of two Liberty & Co. silver frames, Birmingham, 1905, 19.25cm. high.

Silver Art Nouveau photograph frame by J. & A. Zimmerman, 29cm. high, Birmingham, 1903.

PLATES

One of twelve George III dinner plates by Paul Storr, London, 1807, 10½in. diam., 271oz.7dwt.

One of twelve George III shaped circular dinner plates, 9¾in. diam., by L. Herne and F. Butty, London, 1762, 212oz.15dwt.

George I Irish circular plate, 9in. diam., Dublin, 1725, 13oz.13dwt.

One of twelve George II dinner plates, 9¾in. diam., by G. Methuen, London, 1756, 196oz.6dwt.

PORRINGERS

Two-handled George V silver porringer, London, 1915.

Queen Anne porringer on collet foot, 1713, 6oz.

Charles II two-handled porringer, 4½in. high, 13oz. 13dwt.

Charles II plain two-handled porringer on rim foot, probably West Country, maker's mark IP, circa 1670, 6oz. 3dwt.

PURSES

Stylish German silver mesh evening purse, circa 1910, 18cm. long.

Art Nouveau silver purse, 1908.

La Minauderie, silver engine turned evening bag by C. van Cleef and Arpels, about 1935.

18th century Dutch silver gilt bag mount, maker's mark I.V.I., Amsterdam 1749, 3oz. 15dwt.

Queen Anne quaich, by Robt. Ker, Edinburgh, circa 1710.

A typical Stuart quaich, 7¾in. diam., unmarked, Scottish, circa 1675.

One of a small pair of Indian silver quaichs, 7oz.

RATTLES

Victorian silver rattle dated 1886.

Early 18th century child's silver rattle, 5¼in. long, circa 1700.

17th century child's rattle bearing the Edinburgh date letter for 1681.

SALTS

One of a set of four George II capstan salts, London, 1754, by G. Wickes, 32oz.

One of a pair of George III silver salts of spool-shape, London, 1792, 6oz.

One of a pair of late 18th century silver gilt salts, complete with spoons, 23oz.

One of a pair of George III oval salt cellars by Paul Storr, London, 1812, 4½in. wide, 18oz.4dwt.

One of a set of four George III double salts, 4¼in. wide, by J. Scofield, London, 1784, 28oz.15dwt.

One of a pair of Queen Anne trencher salt cellars by B. Bentley, 3in. diam., 4oz.2dwt.

One of a pair of silver salt cellars by Robert Garrard, 3¼in. high.

One of a set of four George III oval tub-shaped silver salts, London, 1808, 12½oz.

SALVERS

George II triangular salver by George Methuen, London, 1752, 16oz.4dwt., 9½in. wide.

Victorian Scottish shaped circular presentation salver, 18in. diam., Edinburgh, 1846, 70oz.18dwt.

George II plain shaped square silver salver, by Robert Abercrombie.

George III shaped circular salver, 11¼in. diam., by J. Carter, London, 1773, 24oz.2dwt.

147

SAUCEBOATS

One of a pair of Victorian sauceboats, 8¼in. long, by Robert Garrard, London, 1847, 41oz.19dwt.

George IV oval sauceboat by E. E. J. & W. Barnard, London, 1829, 7in. wide, 17oz.1dwt.

One of a pair of George II oval sauceboats, by Wm. Cripps, London, 1754, 8in. wide, 28oz.8dwt.

One of a pair of George III oval sauceboats, by Thos. Evans, London, 1775, 34oz. 7dwt., 7½in. wide.

SCISSORS

Silver gilt mounted mother-of-pearl scissor case, circa 1700.

Ornate Victorian silver scissors and matching thimble, Birmingham 1890.

Gilt and silver metal scissors and paper knife, circa 1935.

Tang silver gilt scissors, 7½in. long.

SCOOPS

Silver marrow scoop, by E. B., London, 1745.

Silver Stilton cheese scoop, 1931.

Combined silver marrow scoop and tablespoon, by Elias Cachart, 1750.

Stilton cheese scoop with ejector slide, Joseph Taylor, Birmingham, 1803.

Silver cheese scoop by Mary Chawner, 1840.

Rococo shell heel marrow spoon, George Smith, London, 1780.

SKEWERS

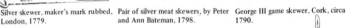

Silver skewer, maker's mark rubbed, London, 1779.

Pair of silver meat skewers, by Peter and Ann Bateman, 1798.

George III game skewer, Cork, circa 1790.

SNUFFERS

George III Irish boat-shaped snuffers tray, by James Scott, Dublin, 8oz. 5dwt.

18th century Dutch silver snuffer stand and snuffers, by Jan Pondt of Bremen, Amsterdam, 1756, 9oz. 18dwt.

Charles II snuffer tray with matching snuffers, by W.B., 15oz.12dwt.

Queen Anne snuffers stand and a pair of snuffers, by Thos. Prichard, London, 1704, 11oz.17dwt.

148

Shaped rectangular silver snuff box with gilt interior by Ed. Smith, Birmingham, 1851, 7.2cm. long.

George III Irish silver snuff box, by A. Tuppy, Dublin, 1782, 3¼in. wide.

A rare late 18th century silver gilt 'mask' snuff box, 3in. wide.

William IV snuff box by Edward Shaw, Birmingham, 1834, 6oz.3dwt., 3¼in. wide.

TANKARDS

George II baluster shaped silver tankard, 1732.

Dutch silver mounted horn tankard with silver lining, with portrait of William and Mary on side.

Queen Anne cylindrical tankard, 8in. high, by Alice Sheene, London, 1709, 30oz. 8dwt.

Silver Augsburg tankard, circa 1700, 33oz., with embosssed decoration.

Early George III tankard, 8in. high, by W.F., London, 1767, 15oz.1dwt.

Tankard given to Bismarck by Wilhelm I of Prussia, 24½in. high, 1871.

Swedish tankard of peg type, repousse decorated with figures and fruits.

George III tapering cylindrical tankard, by Peter and Anne Bateman, London, 1797, 7¼in. high, 26oz.6dwt.

TAPERSTICKS

TAZZAS

George II taperstick, by J. Cafe, London, 1743, 4½in. high, 4oz.7dwt.

Silver taperstick, by E. Barnet, York, 1713, 2¾oz.

18th century Dutch silver gilt tazza, by Casparus Janszonius Haarlem, 4¾in. diam., 3oz.14dwt.

WMF silvered metal tazza, 23.25cm. high, circa 1900.

TEA & COFFEE SETS

Victorian Scottish teaset by Marshall & Sons, Edinburgh, 1849, 40oz.8dwt.

Juventa Art Nouveau electroplated metal coffee service, circa 1900.

Three-piece coffee service by August Dufour, Belgium.

Late Victorian five-piece tea and coffee set by Smith, Sissons & Co., London, 61oz.

Three-piece tea service by Samuel Hennell, London, 1803, 28oz.

Four-piece silver tea service by John Angell, London, 1824.

TEA CADDIES

George III oval tea caddy, 5in. high, by Wm. Vincent, London, 1778, 3oz.10dwt.

George III oblong tea caddy, by P. Gillois, London, 1763, 11oz. 7dwt., 5½in. high.

One of a pair of George II tea caddies, 5¼in. high, by S. Taylor, London, 1756, 16oz.2dwt.

George IV tea caddy, by Charles Price, London, 1828, 18oz.4dwt., 6¼in. high.

George III silver tea caddy, by Rebecca Emes and Edward Barnard I, London, 1809, 22½oz.

One of a pair of George III square tea caddies by R. & S. Hennell, 1803, 26oz.

Silver tea caddy by Paul de Lamerie, 1724, 13.3cm. high, 15oz.13dwt.

One of a pair of George I tea caddies, 5in. high, by G. Roode, London, 1715, 11oz.4dwt.

Bruder Frank kettle and stand, circa 1900, in silver coloured metal.

Victorian silver spirit kettle, by Robb & Whittet, Edinburgh, 1837, 74oz.

George II Irish tea kettle on lampstand, by John Taylor, 13in. high, 67oz.14dwt.

George I tea kettle on stand, 14in. high, by John White, London, circa 1720, 73oz. 9dwt.

TEAPOTS

George III oval teapot by Hester Bateman, 5in. high, London, 1784, 13oz.6dwt.

George III shaped oval teapot and stand, 7in. high, by Langlands & Robertson, Newcastle, 1791, 22oz.

Louis XVI cylindrical teapot, 4in. high, by Jacques Antoine Bonhomme, Paris, 1783, 12oz.11dwt.

Irish George IV silver teapot, Dublin, 1823, by Edward Power, 33oz.

Victorian plated teapot with ivory handle.

Swedish teapot, circa 1819, 21oz., 6in. high.

TOASTERS

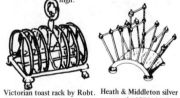

Early Victorian six-section toast rack by Henry Wilkinson & Co., 1839, 8oz.

Victorian six-division silver toast rack, Birmingham, 1898, 9oz.5dwt.

Victorian toast rack by Robt. Garrard, London, 1869.

Heath & Middleton silver toast rack, 1899, 12.5cm. wide.

TOBACCO BOXES

18th century Dutch oblong tobacco box by Christoffel Woortman, Amsterdam, 1797, 6oz.6dwt., 6¼in. wide.

Queen Anne oval tobacco box, by Edward Cornock, London, 1709, 3¼in. wide, 3oz.16dwt.

17th century oval silver tobacco box, 4¼in. wide, circa 1680.

Dutch silver tobacco box, Leeuwarden, circa 1750, 22oz.10dwt.

TOILET REQUISITES

Queen Anne toilet service, London, circa 1706, 81oz.12dwt.

Portuguese silver and stained fish-skin nécessaire de voyage, circa 1730-40.

Fine 19th century dressing case, London, 1838.

TONGS & NIPS

Silver rococo period nips enhanced with gilding, 1745.

Pair of Georgian silver asparagus servers.

George III bright cut sugar tongs, by G. Smith and T. Hayter, London, 1798.

Early 18th century silver sugar tongs, by L.E., London, circa 1710.

Pair of Scottish tongs by Hamilton & Inches, 1906, 48cm. fully extended.

Chased leaf tongs, by W. & J. Deane, London, circa 1765.

Silver asparagus tongs by G. W. Adams, 1864.

Pair of openwork silver tongs by Benjamin Montague, London 1760.

Silver asparagus tongs, by J. Buckett, of London, circa 1770, 23cm. long.

TRAYS

George III two-handled tray, by J. Wakelin and R. Garrard, 1796, 80oz., 20in. long.

Large, heavy Walker & Hall two-handled rectangular tray, Sheffield, 1901, 75.2cm. wide, 5,086gm.

Embossed Indian silver tray, circa 1900, 21in. long.

Late 17th century Dutch spice tray, Rotterdam, circa 1683, 8½in. wide, 5oz.15dwt.

George II shaped triangular tea kettle stand on hoof feet, by R. Abercrombie, 1735, 14oz.11dwt.

Two-handled octagonal pierced gallery tea tray by Elkington & Co., London, 1913, 4,700gm.

152

One of a pair of George III oval sauce tureens and covers, 9¼in. wide, by D. Smith and R. Sharp, London, 1778, 47oz.7dwt.

One of a pair of George III sauce tureens by Wm. Bennett, London, 1808, 52oz.4dwt.

One of a pair of George III silver sauce tureens, by J. Carter, London, 1776, 45oz.

SOUP

Italian lobed circular two-handled soup tureen and cover, 68.5oz., 31.5cm. wide.

George II two-handled soup tureen and cover, Dublin 1745, 164oz., 13¾in. long.

George III oval soup tureen and cover, 15in. wide, by R. Garrard, London, 1814, 121oz.6dwt.

URNS

Early 18th century Scottish urn, 11½in. high, Edinburgh, circa 1725, 43oz.11dwt.

Vase-shaped tea urn, 16¼in. high, by Heath & Middleton, London, 1906, 78oz.4dwt.

George III tea urn, by C. Wright, London, 1771, 80oz.

Unusual George II pear-shaped chocolate urn.

VASES

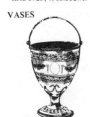

George III sugar vase, by Robt. Hennell, London, 1784, 5in. high, 7oz.9dwt.

Large WMF electroplated electrotype vase, circa 1900, 49cm. high.

Jensen silver vase, London, 1930, 10.25cm. wide.

George III silver gilt covered vase, London, 1770, 20oz.6dwt., 8¼in. high.

VINAIGRETTES

Silver gilt oval vinaigrette by S. Pemberton, Birmingham, 1800.

Early Victorian silver gilt vinaigrette by N. Mills, London, 1838, 1½in. wide.

George IV silver gilt vinaigrette, 1½in. diam., by J. Willmore, Birmingham, 1824.

Silver vinaigrette by J. Butler, Birmingham, 1826.

WINE COOLERS

One of a pair of Catherine the Great wine coolers, by Z. Deichmann, 1766.

One of four George III two-handled campana-shaped wine coolers, 10in. high, 407oz.

One of a pair of George III wine coolers by Paul Storr, London, 1812, 9¾in. high, 242oz.

French vase-shaped wine cooler, 10in. high, circa 1890, 65oz.

WINE FUNNELS

George III wine funnel by George Fenwick, 1817.

George III funnel, by Thos. Graham, London, 1795, 4¼in. high, 1oz.4dwt.

Silver wine funnel by G. Lowe, 1824, 14cm. long.

Georgian silver wine funnel, London, 1811, by E. Morley.

WINE LABELS

George III wine label, engraved for claret, by M. Binley, London, circa 1770.

George IV pierced wine label 'Madeira', by Rawlings & Sumner, 1830.

Rare 18th century wine label apparently unmarked, circa 1780.

Victorian wine label, pierced 'Brandy' by Edward and John Barnard, London, 1853.

WINE TASTERS

William III wine taster, London 1695, 3oz.3dwt.

Mid 17th century wine taster, 4in. diam., 1oz.16dwt.

Charles II circular wine taster, 3¼in. diam., London, 1664, 1oz.18dwt.

Louis XV wine taster with shell thumbpiece, 3¼in. diam., circa 1740, 4oz.4dwt.

154

Lehmann automobile and driver.

19th century model of Noah's Ark in carved wood complete with animals and Noah and his wife.

Lead band of musicians.

Clockwork Steakhouse Joe, made in Japan.

Child's pull-along horse covered with pony skin, circa 1850, 11½in. high.

German Phillip Vielmetter painted tin drawing clown, circa 1900, 5½in. high.

A French automaton of a negro musician from the third quarter of the 19th century, 3ft. high.

A Victorian doll's house with original furniture.

Tinplate clockwork horse and cart, by G. and K. Greppert & Keich, Brandenburg, 17cm. long.

A tinplate clockwork landaulette by Georges Carette, about 1910.

Early 20th century German clockwork clown toy, 9in. high.

Distler clockwork organ grinder, circa 1923, German, 7in. high.

Grizzly bear automaton who moves his legs and bends forward.

Lead set of Snow White and Seven Dwarfs by Britain, 1938.

INDEX

Abercrombie, R. 152
Adams, Charles 133
Adams, G. W. 152
Albarelli 16
Alcock & Co. 27
Aldridge, E. 143
Ale Glasses 105
Aller Vale 26
Angell, John 150
Angell, Joseph 132, 136, 141
Ansbach 16
Apothecary Boxes 105
Argy Rousseau 120
Arita 35
Armoires 53
Augustus, Emperor 21
Austrian China 16

Baccarat 119
Baillie, John 142
Baillie-Scott 81
Baker 45
Barker, Susanna 141
Barnard, E. 128, 132, 145, 148, 150, 154
Barnard, Messrs. 131
Barnet, E. 149
Barnet Fair 32
Barometers 13
Barwise, N. 43
Bateman, Hester 128, 136, 137, 140, 142, 143, 151
Bateman, Peter & Anne 128, 148, 149
Bayreuth 16
Beakers 105, 128
Beauvais, Paul 50
Bebe Bru 52
Beds 54
Beer Jugs 142
Beilby 123
Bell, J. 134
Bellarmine 16
Belleek 16
Bells 105, 129
Bennett, W. M. 153
Benson, W. 51
Berlin 16
Berrolla, Joseph 42
Bible Box 14
Biedermeier 68, 110
Bilbie, E. 45
Binley, M. 154
Biscuit Containers 105, 129
Blue & White China 35
Bloor Derby 21
Bohemian Vases 120

Bonhomme, Jacques 151
Bookcases 55
Bot, Jan 129
Bottger 16
Bottles 106
Boulogne 17
Boulton, Matthew 110
Boulton, Thos. 143
Bow 17
Bowls 106, 129, 130
Boxes 14, 106
Boxwell, Ambrose 142
Bracket Clocks 41
Bragget Pot 19
Brahmfeld, J. F. 140
Brandy Saucepans 131
Breguet a Paris 50
Brewood, Benjamin 131
Bristol 17
Bristol Delft 20
British China 17
Brocard 121
Bronze 13
Bruce, William 142
Bruder, Frank 151
Buckett, J. 152
Buckles 131
Burbridge, R. W. 141
Bureau Bookcases 57
Bureaux 56
Burmantoft 17
Burwash, William 138
Busch, Esajas 128
Butler, J. 154

Cabinets 58
Cachart, Elias 143, 148
Caddies 14, 106
Cafe, J. 132, 149
Cake Baskets 128
Cameras 14
Camerden & Foster 43
Cane Handles 15
Candelabra 107, 131
Candlesticks 107, 132
Canterburys 59
Canton 35
Capodimonte 17
Car Mascots 107
Carafes 107
Card Cases 132
Card & Tea Tables 88
Cardew, Michael 17
Carette, Georges 155
Carriage Clocks 42
Carter, J. 153
Carter, John 136

Carter, Stabler 28
Carved Wood 15
Caskets 132
Castel Durante 17
Castell 18
Casters 133
Caughley 18
Caudle Cups 136
Cellini 141
Ceniers, D. 30
Centrepieces 107, 133
Chairbacks 12
Chairs 60-62
Chalices 133
Chamberlain, Joseph 50
Chamberlain Worcester 34
Chambersticks 133
Champagne Glasses 107
Champions Bristol 18
Chandeliers 108
Chantilly 18
Chawner & Emes 128
Chawner, Henry 128
Chawner, Mary 148
Chelsea 18
Chenghua 35
Chest on Chest 64
Chest of Drawers 63
Chest on Stand 65
Chiffoniers 66
Child & Child 130
China 16-40
Chinese China 35
Chiparus 13
Chocolate Pots 134
Christening Cup 136
Christofle 121
Cigarette Cases 134
Clare, Joseph 135
Claret Jugs 108, 134
Clement 24
Clichy 116
Cliff, Clarice 18
Clock Sets 43
Clocks 41-50
Cloisonne 51
Coalbrookdale 18
Coalport 19
Coasters 134
Coffee Jugs 142
Coffee Pots 135
Coffin, Thos. 142
Cole, Thos. 47
Commemorative China 19
Commode Chests 68
Commodes 69
Coney, John 130

Consol Tables 89
Cope, Erasmus 143
Copeland 19
Copeland & Garret 19
Copeland Spode 19
Coper, Hans 19
Copper & Brass 51
Cordial Glasses 108
Corner Cupboards 70
Cornock, Edward 151
Couches 83
Court Cupboards 70
Cowpe, James 49
Cox & Robinson 105
Cozens, William 41
Cradles 72
Creamboats 135
Cream Jugs 142
Credenzas 73
Cripps, William 135, 148
Crouch, J. 134
Cruets 108, 135
Crump, Francis 130
Cumberworth, Charles 13
Cupboards 74
Cups 108, 136

Daoguang 35
Darker, Wm. 142
Dartmouth 26
Davenport 19
Davenport, Burrage 141
Davenports 75
David & Goliath 47
Davie, William 130
Daum 108, 110, 114, 117, 118, 120
Deacon, John 144
Deane, W. & J. 152
Decanter Boxes 109
Decanters 109
Deck, Theodore 20
Deichmann, Z. 154
Delft 20, 46
Delvaux 118
De Morgan 21
Dent 49
Derby 21
Desks 99
Dickens 22
Dingley, Robert 45
Dining Chairs 60
Dining Tables 90
Dishes 110, 137, 138
Display Cabinets 76
Distler 155
Dixon, James 132

Doccia 21
Dolls 52
Doulton 21, 22
Dresden 22, 43
Dressers 77
Dressing Tables 91
Drinking Glasses 110
Drocourt 42
Drop-Leaf Tables 92
Dr. Wall 34
Dubois 42
Dubot, Jean Francois 81
Dufour, August 150
Duke of York 14
Dumb Waiters 78
Duplessis Pere 130
Dutch China 22
Dutch Delft 20
Dutton, William 41

Earthenware 22
Easy Chairs 61
Edo 35
Edward VII 19
Edwards, J. 137, 142
Egermann, F. 105
Elbow Chairs 62
Eley, William 135, 137
Elkington & Co. 110, 129, 145, 152
Ellicott 50
Emes & Barnard 139
Emes, John 44, 135
English Delft 20
Entree Dishes 137
Epergnes 110, 139
Escritoires 81
European China 22
Evans, Thos. 148
Ewers 111, 139
Exportware 36

Faberge, Carl 143
Fabrication Francaise 52
Faenza 22
Famille Noire 36
Famille Rose 36
Famille Verte 36
Feet 11
Fenwick, George 154
Figures 111
Firing Glasses 111
Fish Servers 139
Fixary, E. 49
Flagons 139
Flasks 111
Flatware 140

Fleming, William 131
Flight, Barr & Barr 34
Forest, Norman 15
Fox, Charles 133, 144
Frankenthal 22
French China 23
Friedemann, C. 48
Friesland Clock 49
Fruit Dishes 138
F.S.S. London 132
Fukagawa 36
Fulham 23

Galle 95, 109, 116, 121
Gallia 145
Games Tables 98
Garrard, R. 137, 148, 151, 153
Garthorne 136
Gateleg Tables 93
George III 28
German China 23
Gibson, John 19
Giffen, Jan Van 141
Gignac, Benjamin 135
Gilbert, Alfred 13
Giles 109, 122
Gillois, P. 150
Gladstone 117
Glass 105-123
Goblets 112, 141
Godfrey, Elizabeth 133
Goelede 15
Goldsmiths & Silversmiths 131
Gorham 139
Gorham, James 48
Gorsuch, Thos. 50
Goss 23
Graham, Thos. 154
Grainger, Worcester 34
Grandfather Clocks 44
Gray, R. 129
Gregory, Mary 105, 109, 111, 113
Greig, David 44
Greppert, G. & K. 155
Groode, Charles 45
Guan 36
Guild of Handicrafts 140, 145

Haan, Cornelis De 129
Haan, Marcelis De 129
Hagenauer 13, 15
Hall, Martin 132
Hall Stands 78
Hamada 36
Hamilton & Inches 152
Hamilton, John 145
Han 36

Hanau 23
Handels 10
Hans Sloane 18
Harlequin 17
Harris, Charles 130, 136
Harrison, Wm. 135
Hawkins, Marke 50
Hayter, T. 152
Hazeldene 26
Heals 101
Heath & Middleton 151, 153
Hennell, R. & S. 133, 134, 135,
150
Hennell, Robt. 128, 144, 153
Hennell, Samuel 150
Henrietta 19
Heron, Robert 32
Heubach 52
Hicht, Sibrand 129
Hichozan 37
Hochst 23
Honey Pots 141
Hot Water Jugs 143
Hougham, Solomon 129
Hozan 37
Hukin & Heath 137
Humpens 112
Hunt, S. 143
Hutton, William 132, 136
Hyde, Mary 145

Icarus 13
Imari 37
Inkstands 112, 141
Inro 14
Instruments 124
Irish Delft 20
Iron 125
Istoriato 31
Italian China 23
Ives & Co. 52
Ivory 125

Jacquemart 50
Jade 126
Jallot, Leon 101
Janszonius, Casparus 149
Japanese China 37
Jardinieres 78
Jars 112
Jennings & Bettridge 80
Jensen 129, 133, 135, 140, 153
Jizhou 35
Johnson 14
Johnson, Glover 133
Jones, George 23
Jouet, Simon 138

Jugs 113, 141, 142, 143
Jumeau 52

Kakiemon 37
Kammer & Reinhardt 52
Kangxi 37
Kayserzinn 138
Keay, R. 143
King, Jessie M. 131
Kinkozan 38
Kipling, Wm. 45
Kirk, Jonah 144
Kneehole Desks 79
Knibb, John 45
Knopfell, F. 131
Knox, John 23
Korean China 38
Kovsch 143
Kutani 38

Ladles 143
Lafayette, General 116
Lalique 46, 107, 108, 109, 111,
112, 113, 115, 116, 121
Lambert & Co. 139
Lambeth Delft 20
Lamerie, Paul de 108, 128, 132,
135, 150
Lamp Shades 114
Lamps 113
Lang Yao 38
Langlands & Robertson 151
Lantern Clocks 45
Large Tables 94
Leach, Bernard 23
Lead 126
Leeds 24
Leeuw Warden 151
Legras 121
Legs 11
Lehmann 155
Lemon Strainers 143
Lepine 50
Levee Du Roi 29
Liao 35
Liberty 47, 51, 83, 130, 131
Library Steps 84
Limoges 24
Liqueur Sets 114
Liverpool 24
Liverpool Delft 21
Loetz 121
London Delft 21
Long, Eliza 33
Longton Hall 24
Lowboys 78
Lowe, G. 154

Lowestoft 24
Ludwigsburg 24
Lustre 24
Lustres 114

McCabe, James 49
Macgillivray 13
Macintyres 24
Mackintosh, Charles Rennie 60,
76, 81, 140
Main, John 135
Majolica 25
Majorelle, Louis 54, 58, 101
Mantel Clocks 46, 47
Mappin & Webb 130, 138, 141
Marble 126
Markwick 50
Marseille 25
Marseille, Armand 52
Marshall & Sons 138, 150
Marti, J. 49
Martin Hall & Co. 142
Martinware 25
Mason's 25
Match-Holders 114
Maurice & Co. 42
Mead Glasses 114
Meat Dishes 138
Meissen 15, 25
Mennecy 25
Menzel, Johann 134
Meriton, Samuel 145
Mettlach 25
Milk Jugs 142
Mills, N. 154
Ming 38
Minton 26
Mirrors 126
Miscellaneous China 38
Miscellaneous Glass 115
Mitchell, John 139
Mitchell, Wm. 44
Mitsouko 118
Mitsuko 118
Models 144
Money Banks 126
Montague, Benjamin 152
Monteith Bowls 130
Moorcroft 26
Morley, E. 154
Motto Ware 26
Mucha 42
Mugs 108, 144
Muller Freres 122
Mulls 144
Mummy Mask 15
Murray, William 26
Musical Boxes 126

Mustards 144
Mysterieuse 50

Nailsea 116
Nankin 39
Nantgarw 26
Naples 26
Narcissus 19
Nefs 145
Negrety 13
Neresheimer, B. 144
Nevers 23
Newhall 27
Nichols & Plinke 134
Nicolle, Louis 140
Niderville 27
Nielson, Nicole 42
Nips 152
Northcote, Francis 143
Nove 27
Nutmegs 145
Nymphenburg 27

Oakley, G. 55
Occasional Tables 95
Ochstenkopf 112
Ohrstrom, Edvin 106
Olding, Nathaniel 77
Oriental China 35
Orrefors 121

Paintbox 14
Phipps & Robinson 145
Panchaud & Cumming 41
Pap Boats 145
Paperweights 116
Parian 27
Paris 27
Peake, Robert 130
Pedestal Desks 79
Pediments 10
Peel, Robert 30
Pekin Vases 122
Pemberton, Samuel 140, 154
Pembroke Castle 31
Pembroke Tables 96
Peppers 145
Persian China 39
Petit, Jacob 27
Pewter 127
Phipps, T. 129
Photograph Frames 146
Pianos 127
Pilkington 27
Pipes 116
Pitchers 116
Pitts, Thos. 139

Plaques 116
Plates 116, 146
Pluto 31
Plymouth 28
Pondt, Jan 148
Pont, Wm. 139
Poole 28
Pootholt, Abraham 130, 141
Pope Leo X 31
Porringers 146
Pot Cupboards 69
Pots 116
Potschappel 28
Prattware 28
Preiss 47
Preist, Wm. 49
Price, Charles 150
Prichard, Thos. 148
Prosperine 31
Punch Bowls 130
Purses 145
Purman, Marcus 133
Putai 15

Qianlong 39
Qing 39
Quaich 147
Quare, Daniel 41
Quiguer, A. 41
Quimper 31

Ramsden, Omar 130, 136, 140
Ratafia Glasses 117
Rattles 147
Ravenscroft 113
Rawlings & Sumner 154
Reco Capey 14
Reid, W. 134
Reily, John 145
Rhinoceros Horn 15
Rhulmann, Jacques 61, 91, 95
Richardson, George 34
Ridgway 28
Rie, Lucy 28
Robb & Whittet 151
Robert & Silva 41
Robin Aux Galeries 44
Robinson, E. 129
Robinson & Leadbetter 27
Rockingham 28
Roemers 117
Roman 28
Romer, Emick 139
Roode, G. 150
Rose Bowls 130
Rosenthal 29
Rosso Antico 32

Royal Copenhagen 29
Royal Crown Derby 21
Royal Doulton 21
Royal Dux 29
Royal Worcester 34
Rozenburg 29
Rummers 117
Ruskin 29
Russel, Gordon 101
Ryozan 39

Sabino 121
Sadler, Robt. 41
Sage, John Le 136
St. Louis 115, 116
St. Paul 29
Saintonage 22
Saltglaze 29
Salts 147
Salvers 147
Samson 29
Sanderson 14
Sarlandie 24
Sarton, Hubert 48
Satsuma 39
Sauceboats 148
Savona 30
Scent Bottles 118
Schlaggenwald 31
Schmit 46
Schuppe, John 142
Scissors 148
Scofield, J. 131
Scoops 148
Scott, James 131, 148
Scott, Walter 19
Screens 80
Secretaire Bookcases 82
Secretaires 81
Sene, Jean Baptiste 86
Settees 83
Settle, T. & J. 132
Sevres 30, 43
S.F.B.J. Paris 52
Sharp, R. 153
Sharp, Robert 135, 142
Shaw, Edward 149
Shaw, William 141
Sheene, Alice 149
Shelves 84
Shibayama 127
Shute, Emma 21
Sicilian 16
Sideboards 85
Side Tables 96
Silver 128-154
Simon & Halbig 52

159

Simpson, P. 19
Simpson, Ralph 19
Sitzendorf 30
Skeleton Clocks 48
Skewers 148
Slipware 30
Smith, Benjamin 128
Smith, D. 153
Smith, Daniel 135
Smith, Edward 132, 149
Smith, G. 152
Smith, Sissons & Co. 150
Smith & Sons 48
Smith, Stephen 133
Smith, William 50
Snow White 155
Snuff Bottles 118
Snuff Boxes 149
Snuffers 148
Sofa Tables 97
Somenova, Maria 143
Song 40
Spencer & Perkins 50
Spode 30
Staffordshire 30, 106, 120
Steiner, Herm 52
Steps 84
Stirn 14
Stirrup Cups 136
Stoneware 31
Stools 86
Storr, Paul 135, 137, 138, 141,
   142, 154
Stourbridge 112, 122
Straus, L. 113
Strutt 47
Sugar Baskets 128
Sugar Bowls 130
Sui 35
Suites 87
Sunderland 31, 117
Susini 13
Sutherland Tables 97
Sutton, Thos. 142
Swansea 31
Sweetmeat Dishes 110, 128, 138
Swiss China 22

Tables 88-99
Tahan, Alexandre 132
Tang 40
Tankards 119, 149
Tanqueray, David 135
Tantalus 119
Tapersticks 119, 149
Tassie 115
Taylor, John 151

Taylor, Joseph 148
Taylor, S. 150
Tazzas 119, 149
Tea Caddy 14, 150
Tea and Coffee Sets 150
Tea Kettles 151
Teapots 151
Teapoys 100
Telephot 14
Terracotta 31
Thierne, Carl 28
Thompson of Kilburn 60
Tiffany 107, 112, 113, 114, 122
Timbrell, Robert 130, 134
Toasters 151
Tobacco Boxes 151
Toilet Requisites 152
Tompion, Thos. 41
Tongs 152
Torcheres 100
Tournai 22
Towel Rails 100
Trays 152
Trunks 67
Tuite, Wm. 128
Tumblers 119, 136
Tuppy, A. 149
Tureens 153
Turner 31
Tuscan 16

Umbrella Stand 100
Urbino 31
Urns 153
Usinger, Heinrich 23

Valadier, Giovanni 133
Van Risen 56 -
Vases 120-122, 153
Vegetable Dishes 138
Venetian 31
Vere & Lutwyche 128
Vielmetter, Phillip 155
Vienna 31
Vinaigrettes 154
Vincennes 32
Vincent, William 150
Viner & Co. 42
Visbagh, Pieter 41
Volkstedt 32
Vyse, Charles 32

Waals, Peter 101
Wakelin & Garrard 138
Wakelin, J. 152
Walford, James 32
Walker & Hall 108, 152

Wall Clocks 49
Wallis & Hayne 140
Walter 115
Wanli 40
Ward, Robert 41
Wardrobes 101
Washstands 102
Watches 50
Waterford 109
Webb 108, 110, 115, 118, 122
Webster, Richard 41
Wedgwood 32
Wei 40
Wemyss 32
Westerwald 32
Whatnots 103
Whieldon 33
White, John 151
Whitfield, Wm. 142
Wichell, Sam 45
Wilkinson, Henry 151
Willaume, David 134
Williams, R. 134, 139
Willmore, J. 154
Windmills, Joseph 45
Windows 122
Wine Coolers 104, 154
Wine Cups 137
Wine Glasses 122
Wine Jugs 143
Wine Labels 154
Wine Toasters 154
Winrowe, Wm. 46
Winter, John 131
Wise, J. 44
Wolff, C. 68
Wollaston, N. 136
Wood, Enoch 33
Wood, Ralph 33
Woodhall, G. 116
Woortman, Christoffel 151
Worcester 33
Workboxes 98
Wright, C. 153
Writing Tables 99
Wrotham 34
Wucai 40
Wynn, Thos. 143

Yixing 40
Yongzheng 40
Yorkshire 34
Yuan 40

Zappler 49
Zurich 34
Zwischengold 106